26-95

67C

Every Manager's Guide to
Human Resource Development

EVERY MANAGER'S GUIDE TO HUMAN RESOURCE DEVELOPMENT

Leonard Nadler
Zeace Nadler

Jossey-Bass Publishers
San Francisco

For sales outside the United States contact Maxwell/Macmillan International Publishing Group, 866 Third Avenue, New York, New York 10022

Printed on acid-free paper and manufactured in the United States of America

 The paper used in this book meets the state of California requirements for recycled paper (50 percent recycled waste, including 10 percent postconsumer waste), which are the strictest guidelines for recycled paper currently in use in the United States.

Library of Congress Cataloging-in-Publication Data

Nadler, Leonard.
    Every manager's guide to human resource development / Leonard Nadler, Zeace Nadler.
        p.   cm. — (The Jossey-Bass management series)
    Includes bibliographical references (p.   ).
    ISBN 1-55542-421-X
    1. Personnel management.   I. Nadler, Zeace.   II. Title.
III. Series.
HF5549.N174   1992
658.3 — dc20   91-36300
                                                                                    CIP

FIRST EDITION
HB Printing   10 9 8 7 6 5 4 3 2 1   *Code 9217*

The Jossey-Bass Management Series

Contents ꎾꎾꎾꎾꎾꎾꎾꎾꎾꎾꎾꎾꎾ

Why Should I Provide HRD Development?   23

Why Should I Be Interested in Making Decisions About HRD?   25

Should We Have HRD Programs?   27

Who Should Attend HRD Programs?   27

How Much Should We Spend?   27

Should We Set Aside Special Space for HRD?   28

Should Managers Be Instructors?   28

How Should I Support Training?   104

What should I be doing in regard to
organizational involvement?

What should I do as part of pre-training?

What should I do during the training?

What is job linkage?

How can I assist in job linkage?

What should I be doing as follow-up?

What Support Should I Give to Education for
My Present Employees?   108

What Support Should I Give to Education for
Employees Who Will Be Coming to Me?   109

What Support Should I Give to
Development?   109

What Support Should I Give to HRD
Consulting?   110

Are There Any Other Ways That I Can
Support HRD?   110

9. **Placing HRD Strategically in the
    Organization**   **111**

Why Should I Be Interested in Where HRD Is
Placed in My Organization?   111

Should There Be One HRD Unit or Many?   111

We Have Never Had An HRD Unit—What
Can I Expect?   112

Why Might I Need an HRD Unit Now, When
There Was Not One Previously?   112

What If an HRD Unit Is Introduced Merely
Because One of Our Executives Made That
Decision?   112

Preface

This book has a specific purpose. It meets a need that arose after our book *Developing Human Resources* ([3rd ed.] San Francisco: Jossey-Bass, 1989) was first published in 1970. Although it was written for HRD practitioners, we found that it appealed to non-HRD people. Sometimes it happened that HRD people passed the book on to their managers. Other times, non-HRD managers found the book for themselves and wanted to apply the concepts to their organization.

As a result, we were frequently urged to write a second book, addressed this time to non-HRD managers. We did so, and the book was published under the title *Corporate Human Resource Development* (New York: Van Nostrand Reinhold, 1980). After years of consulting work in the HRD field, it became apparent that there was a considerable amount that non-HRD managers needed and wanted to know that was not included in either of our first two books. Consequently, we decided to write a book focusing specifically on what non-HRD managers have told us that they want to know.

Audience

The audience for this book will be essentially the same as for our last book — namely, managers from the supervisory level to the executive level who do *not* have HRD as their major responsibility. These are the people who have been the main focus of our workshops and our consulting work. Given the overlap between the different levels of supervisors, managers, and executives, we have chosen to use the word *manager* as the generic term for all those groups.

Even though this book is written for non-HRD people, that does not mean HRD people should not be interested in it. On the contrary, we urge HRD people to read this book and then consider placing copies in the hands of their various managers. We have frequently found in the course of our own activities that non-HRD managers appear more likely to accept these ideas from somebody outside their own organization.

The format of this book reflects our own experiences working with non-HRD managers. In our work we have found it more useful to encourage questions than to present information, ideas, or concepts. Of course, a bit of that was necessary to provide a framework, but afterwards we just let the questions come. After a while, we began saving questions, particularly those that arose again and again in a wide variety of settings. It is for this reason that we decided to put this book in a question-and-answer format. Most of the questions are those we have been asked, and the rest are those that were implied. The table of contents is constructed to serve as an index to these questions, which are the key topics of the book.

One big difference between this book and our earlier ones is the reflection of new trends in the workplace and in HRD. A very strong trend is for organizations to assign general managers to head up HRD units. At first, HRD people saw this as a criticism of HRD or as an assessment that HRD was not important (because anybody could do it). Neither of these assumptions is true. In fact, we found that this trend reflects increased organizational respect for HRD. Organizations appoint non-HRD managers to run HRD because they feel HRD can be enhanced by having a non-HRD manager temporarily in charge. From this experience, the non-HRD manager can get a better idea of what HRD can contribute to the success of an organization and can apply that understanding in future assignments in other parts of the organization.

In many organizations that still put a professional HRD person in charge of HRD, the way HRD is organized has changed. There is less emphasis on the need for a large HRD staff to deliver programs and more emphasis on utilizing line personnel (managers and nonmanagers) in designing and delivering HRD programs. Therefore, the line managers need to know much more about what HRD is and what it can do. This book should also prove helpful to them.

Overview of the Contents

Because this book is written in a question-and-answer format, our comments here will focus on the general direction and content of the questions.

Chapter One provides an overview of human resources, including such areas as human resource management, human resource environment, organizational development, employee assistance programs, and quality of work life. Special attention is given to human resource development (HRD), as that is the main focus of this book. A distinction is made between the three main HRD activities of training, education, and development. Note is also taken of miscellaneous areas such as human resource planning, industrial-labor relations, human resource research, and career development. To a manager who has little experience with human resources, these terms can sound quite confusing. The material in this chapter sorts out the principal terms and activities one finds in the human resource field.

There is also material in this chapter that highlights why every manager should be interested in HRD and what it can do for an organization in such areas as productivity, performance appraisals, internal mobility, employee satisfaction, succession planning, customer service, mergers and acquisitions, and strategic planning. The chapter concludes by answering questions about what one can expect when assigned to be a manager of HRD and why it is not necessary to be an HRD expert in order to manage the function.

In Chapter Two, the three key activity areas — training, education, and development — are explored in more depth. The chapter starts by indicating how HRD provides help to organizations and to individual managers. This is followed by some material related to training (focus on present job), such as dealing with performance deficiencies, introducing new products and processes, and providing the learning needed when new policies are introduced in the organization.

This chapter continues with some material on education

(focus on future job), such as planning for promotions, lateral transfers, upswings and downturns in the organization, downsizing, and the relationship of HRD education to career development.

The third area, development (not job related), is also explored. This area of learning is difficult for some people to grasp since it does not relate directly to job performance. Therefore, the discussion clarifies why it is necessary to provide development. Other topics covered include learning readiness, unforeseen organizational changes, and development as a sign of concern for employees.

The chapter then moves to a discussion of why all managers should be involved in HRD decisions about staffing, funding, and facilities for HRD. The question of where HRD should be placed in the organization is also discussed here. The chapter ends with a discussion of why HRD is needed and who should benefit from it.

Chapter Three provides managers with important information about what HRD people do and asks questions related to staffing the HRD unit. This is particularly important as the type of staff will affect the kinds of services a manager can expect.

The next series of questions relates to the roles that HRD practitioners play. The roles (and sub-roles) discussed include manager of HRD (supervisor of HRD programs, developer of HRD personnel, arranger of facilities and funding, maintainer of interpersonal relations), learning specialist (instructor, designer of HRD programs, developer of instructional strategies), and consultant (only touched on briefly here as the following chapter focuses on this role and its sub-roles).

The chapter goes on to look at how many people should be in the HRD unit and whether HRD people are professionals. A differentiation is made between the three types of people involved in HRD: the professionally identified (Category I), for whom HRD is their professional field; the organizationally identified (Category II), for whom the organization is the major focus and who expect to be moved to different jobs within the organization; and those who have collateral HRD duties (Category III) — that is, managers who are involved in some HRD activities.

There is no implication that any one of these is better than another. Rather, what is explored is the question of when one type of person (category) is more helpful than another. As a manager, you can expect to be asked to assign some of your staff (Category II or III) to HRD operations at different times, and the benefits and losses of such assignments are indicated.

As the term *consultant* is used quite freely by many people, Chapter Four starts by defining a consultant and then presents the reasons you might want to use an HRD consultant. This is followed by material on what to look for in a consultant, on choosing and using consultants, and on what HRD consultants do.

A major emphasis is on the relationship between the consultant (HRD practitioner) and the client (manager). Both parties have expectations of the relationship that need to be explored and clarified. When you (a manager) use a consultant, it is much different from merely acquiring an additional employee. Among other things, it is important to know when it ends. Indeed, the ending of a consulting relationship needs some kind of ritual so that all parties know that the relationship has been completed.

This chapter also looks at the two main kinds of consultants in HRD: content consultants and process consultants. Whether you obtain your consultants from your own organization's HRD unit or from the outside, you can expect them to function in one or more of the following sub-roles: expert, advocate, stimulator, and change agent. Knowing these different possibilities can help you in selecting and using the appropriate HRD consultant. This applies whether that consultant is internal or external. When seeking external consultants, a factor to be considered is whether you want an individual consultant or a group of consultants.

As with any activity, resources are needed for HRD, and Chapter Five addresses the need to provide funding and facilities for HRD. There is some discussion of centralized and decentralized HRD operations. This is followed by an examination of the three main financing structures for HRD: budget-item centers, cost centers, and profit centers. The choice must, of course, be consistent with your organization's financial policies regarding HRD and similar functions.

HRD frequently requires dedicated space, including space for general sessions, small group sessions, use of computers and allied instructional devices, and hands-on learning experiences for skill aspects of jobs. This space may be right in your own work space, in a different part of the organization, or totally outside the organization.

A recent trend has been for organizations to develop a corporate conference center that houses centralized HRD programs as well as facilities for other kinds of learning and for meetings. As a manager, you may be placed in charge of such a center, or you may be called upon to discuss whether your organization needs such a center.

As with any other unit, the HRD function must keep records of its use of facilities and funding. There are times when you may need to become familiar with these records in order to make suggestions and decisions regarding HRD.

As HRD is essentially concerned with learning, the discussion in Chapter Six of employee learning and performance improvement is important for managers. Indeed, all managers should know something about the learning they are expected to provide, either on the job or by sending an employee away from the job site for HRD. Although a manager need not be an expert on learning, every manager should be familiar with the basic concepts of andragogy (adult learning), including such factors as intent to apply the learning, prior experience, and self-direction. There are a wide variety of instructional strategies (methods, techniques) and materials that can be used; managers should be familiar with the common ones. In addition, given the impact of technology, managers should be familiar with computer-assisted instruction — what it is and what it can do, as well as what it cannot do. Other instructional strategies and materials discussed include the video disk (high technology) and job aids (low technology).

Chapter Seven, which focuses on evaluation of HRD programs and activities, is vital for all managers. HRD costs money and time, and you want to know what you have gotten in return, or what it would cost you if you did not provide

HRD. The word *evaluation* can produce uncomfortable feelings, but it need not. There are experts who can help you evaluate HRD, but the basic decisions as to what you want to find out about HRD rest with you. As most of HRD is concerned with performance, that becomes an essential element in most HRD evaluations.

This brings us to two different kinds of data that you must consider: hard and soft. Hard data are concerned with presenting actual numbers (for example, dollars or units of production) and can be used where you regularly assess performance in those terms. Soft data are concerned with nonquantifiable factors (for example, relationships or quality of performance) and may be more useful in assessing behavioral changes.

The distinctions made between the HRD activities (training, education, and development) are crucial in getting good evaluation information. Generally, you will be concerned most with evaluating training, and that is discussed more fully than the other two activities.

Your HRD unit needs to know when you want the evaluation to take place and what you intend to do with the results. That will give the HRD staff the necessary information to plan the type and time of evaluation.

As with other activities, HRD cannot exist without support, which is the topic of Chapter Eight. After a discussion of why you, a non-HRD manager, should be interested in supporting HRD, the chapter looks at the kinds of support you might give. The focus is on support of training programs through four stages: pre-training, training, job linkage, and follow-up.

It is not possible to use the same model for education without some significant modifications. However, there are some specific activities you can be involved in when supporting education and development that are briefly described.

As more and more organizations develop HRD units or expand existing ones, the placement of HRD in the organization increases in importance. Every manager must be interested in where HRD is located in the organization. As Chapter Nine illustrates, there are many alternatives. Expanding an existing HRD function is not the same as introducing the function where it did not previously exist.

Part of the answer to the general question of placement focuses on the kinds of HRD programs that managers expect to have available. This becomes an issue even when the HRD unit is not new and is not being expanded. Organizational values and culture came under close scrutiny during the last years of the 1980s, and it can be expected that this activity will continue, as well it should. It should also be recognized that HRD can have an important impact on organizational values and culture.

The perennial question of whether HRD should be centralized or decentralized is addressed here. While there is no one correct choice, several alternatives are discussed at some length. There is also a series of questions on placement of an HRD function within the unit you manage. This appears to be an increasing trend as it brings the development and delivery programs right into the units that need it.

Because there are many professional and ethical issues related to HRD, they are discussed separately, in Chapter Ten. For example, what right does an organization have to try to change an employee's behavior? What about using HRD to present controversial material? Is HRD a form of brainwashing or therapy?

One concept of employment in the United States considers employees as volunteers. What does this mean with respect to HRD? Although the number of union members in the U.S. work force has been decreasing, unions are still a significant factor for many organizations. What is the relationship between HRD and unions?

Organizations have increasingly come to understand that they must be involved with the communities in which they are located. A prime example is the relationship of business to local school systems. HRD certainly has a place in this relationship, but it must be explored carefully. This is particularly evident in programs concerned with what is called cooperative education.

HRD also has a role to play in the pressures that arise from changing economic conditions or from special populations such as ethnic minorities, women, immigrants, and so on. There is also the recognition that changing demographics, particularly those related to age, can have an enormous impact on an organization. Here also there is a role for HRD. As HRD becomes more of a national concern, we are likely to see an increase in HRD-related legislation. As this happens, it will no longer be possible to consider HRD a fringe area.

An increasing number of organizations are concerned about the global aspects of doing business. This concern is the focus of Chapter Eleven. There are certain specific areas where HRD must be involved, such as in sending employees to work overseas. Even when employees are already working overseas, there are many areas where HRD can be helpful.

All too often the assumption is made that it is easy to return to the United States after working overseas. Unfortunately, that is not necessarily true, and employees in that situation can certainly benefit from well-organized HRD programs.

If your organization has operations in other countries, then HRD must be considered from yet another perspective. There are many political and social implications of HRD programs, in addition to the obvious economic ones. Some U.S. organizations have tried to meet local HRD needs outside the United States by just shipping over materials produced here. In many situations, those materials are useless, and they may even be counterproductive.

Once again, you must look at the differences between training, education, and development to see how each can best be used in international operations, either in the United States or abroad. For example, many U.S. companies in developing countries are expected to provide special kinds of scholarships, but unless these relate specifically to HRD objectives they may be a waste of money.

Another important consideration is the so-called levy system, which exists in many countries (the United States is an exception) to raise money for HRD by taxing payrolls. As HRD is heavily involved in such a system, it is important to know what it is and exactly how HRD relates to it.

In the last chapter we take a look at the future of HRD. It is impossible to cover all the implications for the future because the future keeps changing. There are, however, some areas in which the implications for the future are fairly obvious. These include changes in the structures of organizations, lack of literacy in the work force, immigration, the information explosion, the rate of technological change, and the one-world concept.

Acknowledgments

Although it is traditional to acknowledge those who have made significant contributions to a book such as this one, we hesitate to do so, for the list would be very long. It would include our clients, particularly the managers whose questions are reflected in this book. There would have to be a long list of managers from many companies and many parts of the world who took part in the various workshops we conducted over the years. Then, we would have to add the individuals who were not clients or participants but with whom we discussed some of these questions. That would include the students who were in our classes at The George Washington University.

Rather than a list, therefore, we hope all will accept this general acknowledgment and our thanks for their help in raising questions and clarifying ideas.

College Park, Maryland   Leonard Nadler
December 1991   Zeace Nadler

The Authors

Leonard Nadler is a partner in Nadler Associates and professor emeritus of the School of Education and Human Development, The George Washington University, where he developed the graduate program in human resource development. He received his B.B.A. degree (1948) in accounting from the City College of New York, his M.A. degree (1950) in business education from the City College of New York, and his Ed.D. degree (1962) in educational administration from Teachers College, Columbia University.

His major activities have been developing concepts and models in the field of human resource development. He has worked with a wide variety of clients, in both the private and public sectors, throughout the United States and in more than thirty foreign countries. He has received numerous awards, including an honorary Doctor of Humane Letters from the National College of Education (1988) and the first Distinguished Contribution to HRD Award (1986) from the American Society for Training and Development (ASTD), has been elected to the HRD Hall of Fame (1987) of *Training Magazine,* and has been chosen as one of the ten outstanding trainers by the readers of *Training Magazine.* He is the author of over 150 articles published in various professional publications and several books, including *Professional Skills of the Manager* (1988), *Managing Human Resource Development* (1986, with G. Wiggs), *Clients and Consultants: Meeting and Exceeding Expectations* ([2nd ed.] 1985, with C. Bell), *The Handbook of Human Resource Development* (1984, editor), *Designing Training Programs* (1982), and *Corporate Human Resource Development* (1980).

Zeace Nadler is a partner in Nadler Associates. She received her B.A. degree (1946) in English literature from Brooklyn College. She has taught in the HRD program at The George Washington University and worked with her husband, Leonard, in his HRD assignments both in the United States and abroad. She has helped many authors get published and has helped edit all of the articles and books written by Leonard.

Together, Leonard and Zeace Nadler have written several articles and authored *The Comprehensive Guide to Successful Meetings and Conferences* (1987) and *The Conference Book* (1977). They both also serve as consulting editors to Jossey-Bass Publishers in the area of HRD, as well as for *The Trainer's Resource* (HRD Press), and for the Releasing Human Potential Series (Gulf Publishing).

EVERY MANAGER'S GUIDE TO HUMAN RESOURCE DEVELOPMENT

What Human Resource Development Is and Is Not

Why Was This Book Written?

We have written several books on human resource development (HRD) that were addressed essentially to the HRD practitioner. For many years, however, we have also conducted workshops on HRD for non-HRD managers and have consulted with those managers about HRD. From those experiences it became clear that many general managers felt a need for a concise book on HRD so that they could see both how HRD relates to their function (their duties and responsibilities) and how to use HRD as a management tool.

In our work with managers, we found it helpful to obtain the questions that they wanted to ask of their HRD people. In working with HRD practitioners, we collected questions that they wished their managers would ask them. These two sets of questions are the basis for this book and the reason we have chosen to set up this book in a question-and-answer format. We believe that this approach can be very helpful in enabling you, as a manager, to select those specific areas that are of concern at a particular time, without having to read the whole book at once. This book can serve as a continuing resource for you — as a manager's guide to human resource development.

There is also the possibility that at some point in your career as a manager you will be called upon to be the manager of an HRD unit. Throughout this book there is material that could be helpful to you in such an event, but that possibility will also be addressed in a specific question later in this chapter.

1

The questions are generally phrased as they have been (or would be) asked by a non-HRD manager.

What Does the Word *Manager* Mean in This Book?

In the United States there is no absolute agreement on who is and is not a manager. There is some general agreement, however, and we will endeavor to clarify it here—at least for the purposes of this book.

The first level of management is the *supervisor,* sometimes called the first-line manager. It is the first level of an organization, where people get the work done through the efforts of others. It is not possible to delineate the kinds of decisions supervisors make, as that generally varies from one company to another. Indeed, it can even vary within the same organization.

A *manager* is essentially a person who supervises a supervisor. There can be several levels of managers, but there has been an increasing tendency to reduce the number of middle-level managers. There are different kinds of managers (as discussed under the next question) who differ in what they manage, rather than in level.

At some place in the organization, the manager blends into the *executive.* Generally, there is no absolute way to determine at what level in the organization this shift takes place. It used to be clear when one became an executive because this was when one received the key to the executive washroom and a seat in the executive dining room. Due to significant changes in the workplace, these can no longer be used as indicators of who is an executive. While the designation of this level is peculiar to each organization, the CEO (chief executive officer) and the president are clearly always executives. There may be some indications about who else the organization considers an executive. Among the possible indicators are inclusion in the profit-sharing arrangement, permission to purchase stock, and selected perks such as an automobile or an expense account.

For the purposes of this book, the term *manager* will generally be used to include all three levels: supervisor, manager, and executive. At times, when it is desirable to be less general, a specific level will be indicated.

What Does a Manager Manage?

The general tendency is to think of managers as people who manage other people. That is not always the case. There are managers who manage time, space, resources, and other aspects of business and industrial life. There is no contention, in this book, that the manager of people is better than other managers, but certainly the people manager tends to be different. This becomes apparent when a manager of space is moved into a position where he or she is required to manage people.

This book is directed mainly to those who manage people. That is not to say that other managers should not be concerned with HRD. The manager of financial resources (comptroller, treasurer, accountant) as well as the manager of physical resources (plant, office) are also involved in providing resources for HRD. From time to time there will be some material that is important for them.

The job of the manager is to enable an organization to achieve its goals and mission through the effective utilization of resources, and the human resource cannot be overlooked.

What Is Meant by Human Resources (HR)?

This is the generic name that has been given to all those areas of the work relationship where people are involved. At this point, let us look at the broad area of human resources, not just at human resource *development*. For those who have been in management for a long time, the term *human resources* may seem strange, as it did not appear until about 1970. It has slowly replaced such limited terms as *personnel* and *manpower*. This is more than just a semantic change; it is a change signifying a new emphasis on seeing people as one of the most important resources of an organization.

How Can Humans Be Considered a Resource?

There are those who argue that human beings cannot be a resource, but we feel this is too narrow a view. Obviously, the human resource should not be considered the same as a physical resource or financial resource. Each resource has its own idiosyncrasies that a manager must consider. In particular, it should be recognized that managing the human resource includes having a philosophy about people and their personal values.

What Is Included in the Field of Human Resources?

There are many ways to group the human resource functions in an organization, and the groupings discussed below should not be seen as absolutes. The groupings here are designed to enable managers to make some sense out of this burgeoning area of organizational activity.

The major human resource groupings are management, environment, development, and other. The last group is admittedly a catchall for different types of activities related to human resources that have not yet emerged into a major grouping or are slowly changing or disappearing.

What Is Human Resource Management?

Human resource management includes recruitment, selection, placement, compensation, and appraisal of employees; development of information systems; and determination of employee benefits. These are the activities that were the core of the personnel function in the past. They are still basic, though the emphasis keeps shifting in the wake of new legislation (for example, equal employment opportunity laws). Certainly, the introduction of the computer has given added emphasis to the development of personnel information systems. It is interesting to note that in 1989 the American Society for Personnel Administration changed its name to the Society for Human Resource Management.

What Is Human Resource Environment?

Human resource environment includes organizational development, employee assistance programs, and quality of work life. These activities, each of which may well be a separate unit within the organization, have emerged more recently in human resource history and can be expected to be with us for a long time. They are discussed separately and in more detail below.

What is organizational development? Organizational development is difficult to define, as many definitions have evolved since this became a very active area in the early 1970s. David Nadler, a leading organizational development practitioner, has defined it as "a planned and systematic attempt to change patterns of organizational behavior" (*Feedback and Organization Development: Using Data-Based Methods.* Reading, Mass.: Addison-Wesley, 1977, p. 3). The goal of the efforts is to make an organization more effective through various activities usually termed *interventions.* These can be structural — that is, focused on the way the activity is organized. They can also involve activities that focus on people, usually in groups.

What are employee assistance programs? Employee assistance programs are company activities that help employees in their personal lives, particularly as related to their jobs. They started as a reaction to the use of drugs in the workplace, as it became apparent that workdays were being lost and there was a danger of increased accidents, some of which could be disastrous. The programs were extended to include alcoholism and then obesity and smoking. Of course, there are value judgments involved in identifying these as problem areas, and the programs themselves raise the issue of privacy. A consensus has emerged, however, that some attention needs to be given to these areas. A more positive approach has emerged as the emphasis in employee assistance programs has shifted to health and fitness. Large organizations have built special facilities for this, while small organizations have often made arrangements with local spas or other health facilities. Employee assistance programs appear to be gaining popularity in part because of the graying of the work force and the need for care for the older parents of those still in the work force.

What is quality of work life? The underlying concept of quality of work life is that as we spend so much of our daily time at work, consideration should be given to making the workplace as attractive as possible. This concept has many dimensions and goes far beyond just painting the walls or providing parking space. It involves the whole work environment — the human as well as the physical.

What Is Human Resource Development (HRD)?

There are several different definitions of HRD, but we prefer our own definition, which we first stated in a slightly different form in 1970. In our view, human resource development can best be defined as "organized learning provided by employers within a specified period of time to bring about the possibility of performance improvement and/or personal growth."

Within HRD there are three different kinds of learning programs, based on job focus. They are training, education, and development.

What is training? Training is the activity where the learning is focused on the *present job* of the learner.

What is education? Education is the activity where the learning is focused on a *future job* for the learner.

What is development? Development is the activity where the learning does *not* focus on a job.

Does Training Cover All Three Activity Areas?

There is an unfortunate tendency to use the word *training* to mean all three, and that results in a loss of focus and affects objectives and evaluation. Throughout this book we will only use "training" to mean learning for the present job of the learner. As you will see, it makes a great deal of difference whether the objective is training, education, or development. (A fuller discussion of these three activity areas of HRD is contained in Chapter Two.)

What Are Some of the Other Human Resource Areas?

These areas include human resource planning, industrial-labor relations, research, and career development. These are generally areas that are either changing or emerging. They are examined in more detail below.

What is human resource planning? At one time human resource planning was part of human resource management. It consisted mainly of succession planning and recruitment, but it has slowly become recognized that human resource planning goes far beyond that. This has been highlighted by the demographic changes in our work force, notably the shortage of young people for entry-level jobs and the changing legal requirements for retirement.

The most common forms of succession planning are concerned with keeping track of positions and of people in the organization who might fill them. This must be coordinated with programs that provide employees with appropriate experiences (assignments and learning) so that they are ready to move into identified positions as such positions open up.

What is industrial-labor relations? Industrial-labor relations usually refers to union-management affairs. At one time that was a major aspect of the human resource field, but it has become less significant as the number of unionized workers has decreased. It is still important, however, in those organizations that are unionized.

What is human resources research? At one time, human resources research was mainly related to establishing wages, but it has since expanded as organizations have discovered the need to find out much more about the human resource and what affects it. Large organizations such as AT&T have a whole unit devoted to human resources research. Small organizations tend to use outside resources when a research need arises, such as identifying the reasons for employee turnover or the level of employee satisfaction.

What is career development? Career development was, at one time, a part of human resource management. In many organizations it has become a separate unit in recognition of the fact that career development goes far beyond just trying to find out what job is next (Leibowitz, Z. B., Farren, C., and Kaye, B. L. *Designing Career Development Systems.* San Francisco: Jossey-Bass, 1986). Career development and HRD are related in many ways, but they require different competencies in the individuals doing those jobs. It is important, however, that the career development system and the HRD system be interactive (Gutteridge, T. G., and Hutcheson, P. G. "Career Development." In L. Nadler and Z. Nadler [eds.], *The Handbook of Human Resource Development.* [2nd ed.] New York: Wiley, 1990).

Why Is There So Much Confusion About Human Resource Terms?

For many years, some managers considered human resources less important than physical and financial resources. As interest in human resources has grown, different people and disciplines have moved into the picture, each carrying its own terminology. For example, some people call the total operation human resources, while others call it human resource management. That is why the previous questions are important, at least to understanding this book. We shall restrict the term *human resource management* to just the personnel functions listed earlier and use *human resources* when referring to all the human resource functions.

How Should Human Resources Be Organized Within a Company?

There is no one best way to organize human resources and probably never will be. Each organization will have to consider how to group these functions based on its own organizational needs. These groupings will also be influenced by the history of the organization. For example, if career development has been under human resource management, separating those activities out may prove to be painful and disruptive. The result might be a power fight, which would not be helpful to anybody. Therefore, managers may decide to retain the existing organization of human resources even if a change could mean an improvement.

The groupings will also be influenced by the people in each human resource area. Each area requires specialized competencies, and it is impossible to find one individual today who possesses all the competencies required in the human resource field. Some services, such as recruitment, might be accomplished by contracting with an external company. This would, of course, influence how the human resource operation is organized in a particular company.

Why Should I Be Interested in Human Resources?

As a manager, you probably feel that you are so busy with your own work that you would just as soon leave human resources to the professionals. This approach is becoming less and less desirable. Assuming the human resource professionals are good — and most of them are — they still need the help of general line managers. After all, the basic reason for the existence of human resource professionals is to serve you and other managers, and they cannot do this without your help and guidance.

As a manager utilizing human resources, you should know how the need for them is determined in the organization, where the human resources come from, and what people expect when they join your organization. Human resources are too important to be left to the professionals alone.

Is HRD Something New?

HRD is probably as old as the existence of people on this earth, since from the earliest times it has been necessary for people to learn the competencies needed for survival. Obviously, those competencies have changed over the millennia. For the purposes of this book it is important to recognize that when people came together in one place for production, in what was the factory of the late 1700s, something took place that has been labeled the industrial revolution. This gave rise to programs to teach employees so that they could become effective workers (and later supervisors and managers). By the end of the nineteenth century there were specialized activities related to those learning programs that were readily identifiable. The HRD field has grown ever since, slowly for the most part but with spurts during the two world wars.

More recently, the early 1970s saw an increasing awareness of the need for learning programs for employees, and the number of people in the HRD field rapidly increased. By the early 1990s it was possible to see that almost any organization of one hundred employees or more had some form of HRD program.

Why Should I Be Interested in HRD?

As a manager, you are constantly called upon to solve problems, and for some of them HRD can be an appropriate response. Using HRD effectively can make your job easier and contribute to your success. This does not require that you become a specialist in HRD, but it does require that you know enough about it to be able to make the necessary managerial decisions. This book is designed to give you the background to facilitate your decision making where HRD is concerned.

What Kinds of Decisions Have HRD Implications?

Some of the decisions you make may not seem to have HRD implications until looked at closely. Opening a new facility, closing an old one, expanding or contracting operations, venturing into new markets — all of these changes involve human resources, people who will have to possess the competencies required to implement your managerial decisions. If your work force is to be ready when needed, it is important that you involve the HRD people early enough so they can put the learning programs online promptly.

How Can HRD Help Me, As a Manager?

HRD can be a good tool for a manager, but in order to use it effectively, you have to know what it is and what it can do for you and your organization. You could ask the HRD people in your organization, but they may not have the background to give a solid answer, and they may not be familiar with the entire HRD field. If they are, consider yourself very fortunate, for you will be able to discuss specific questions and responses in this book with them.

As a manager, you want your people to be not only competent (able to do what they are assigned to do) but working at their highest level of excellence. There are many ways to reach for excellence in performance, and one of them is to provide the appropriate learning at the optimum time. A good HRD program can give you this management tool.

What Can HRD Do for My Organization?

This is an important question and one that is going to require a rather lengthy response, as there are so many areas that involve HRD. Among the areas to be discussed here are productivity, performance appraisal, internal mobility, employee satisfaction, succession planning, customer service, mergers and acquisitions, and corporate strategic planning. This brief list by no means exhausts the possibilities.

The following comments on these areas are being kept short because some of them are developed much more in later portions of this book.

How does HRD relate to productivity? There are many definitions of productivity, but one that we have found helpful comes from John G. Belcher, Jr., of the American Productivity Center. He defines productivity as "the relationship between the output of an organization and its required inputs" (*Productivity Plus: How Today's Best-Run Companies Are Gaining the Competitive Edge.* Houston, Texas: Gulf Publishing, 1987, p. 3).

It is possible to increase output (either goods or services) by increasing input — by buying more machines, say, or hiring more people. However, that is not an increase in *productivity* but an increase in *production*. An improvement in productivity is signified by increasing output *without* increasing input.

Training can make a significant contribution to improving output in the present, particularly where it deals with those activities that are directly related to improving the input-output ratio. *Education* may have a similar impact, but only in the future, when the employee is able to apply his or her learning on the new job. *Development* cannot be expected to produce any improvement in productivity because the learning it entails is not related to a specific job, present or future.

How does HRD relate to performance appraisal? When you, as a manager, complete the performance appraisal of one of your subordinates, there is usually an HRD component. If the employee is not working at an acceptable level, what is the reason? If the employee does not know how to perform the work at the standard you require, then training is needed. If the employee is working well and you note something like "this employee has potential," then you should be providing the appropriate education to assist the employee to reach that potential.

How does HRD relate to internal mobility? Internal mobility is the term for employees moving from one part of your organization to another, usually to a different job. HRD can provide a means to assist in this mobility. Through education, it is possible to provide an opportunity for an employee to learn about other jobs in the organization, as well as a chance to try out the job during the learning process.

Can HRD contribute to employee satisfaction? It has been suggested that HRD can contribute to employee satisfaction, though there is little hard evidence to support this contention. Presumably, when an organization provides HRD, employees will take this as a sign that management is interested in them as individuals, not just for what they can contribute to the success of the company. This is certainly a possibility when development is offered; however, it may be less true for training and education.

How can HRD contribute to succession planning? An obvious contribution that HRD can make to an organization is in facilitating succession planning. In some organizations, a manager cannot expect to be promoted until a replacement has been identified and educated. Therefore, HRD can contribute to your promotional possibilities when you provide education for employees who are part of the succession plan.

How does HRD relate to customer service? There has been an increasing concern over improving customer service, and HRD is one way of meeting that concern. Many people in the work force today did not receive any instruction (training or education) in how their jobs relate to customer service. It is possible to put a training program in place that will help employees realize how their activities relate to your organization's customer service policy and that will provide them with skills in that area.

Does HRD have a role to play in mergers and acquisitions? Mergers and acquisitions are activities that swell and wane but seem to be always with us. They involve much more than just a reallocation of financial and physical resources. The human resource is very much involved, too, and the whole process can be enhanced by providing appropriate training and education programs prior to the merger or acquisition, as well as after.

What is strategic planning? There are several different definitions of strategic planning, but the one we have found most helpful states that it is a *questioning process* an organization must consistently engage in over many years. As a concept, it is still very new, having only emerged with any force in the early 1980s. It is *not* long-range planning, though that is often confused with strategic planning. Good strategic planning *leads to* effective long-range planning.

     In strategic planning, some of the questions that are asked are: What business should we be in? What should be the driving force in our organization? Who should be our customers or clients? The search for the answers to these questions is a collaborative effort by a group composed of people from different parts of the organization.

How Can HRD Assist Me and My
Organization in Doing Strategic Planning?

You will benefit by involving your HRD people during the strategic planning process because they can begin to plan for the kinds of HRD programs that will help you reach your identified strategic goals. Engaging in the strategic planning process may mean that your people will need to learn skills in working together in small groups, in identifying problems and opportunities, and in "futuring."

My Organization Is Constantly
Changing. How Can HRD Help?

There are several ways HRD can help in a changing environment, and one of them is to keep your work force in a constant state of learning readiness (more on this in Chapter Six). More specifically, through HRD you can help your people learn how to deal with the stress and anxiety that come with any change. There are known techniques which would be extremely helpful to them and to you, both before and during a transition.

What If I Am Assigned to Be the Manager of HRD?

There are managers who consider running HRD to be the kiss of death. Being assigned as the HRD manager may be construed as being shunted off to the side or to a position that nobody really wants. At one time that may have been true, but it is certainly no longer the case. Given the increased concern about human resources, being assigned to any human resource function can be an important part of a manager's career path.

It is important to see how such an assignment relates to the general practice for managers in your organization. In most organizations, moving middle managers at least every five years is a general practice. Although the HRD assignment may seem to be out of the direct production or service areas of your organization, it has many values. People in HRD can work with *all* parts of an organization, so in this assignment you will become familiar with parts of the organization you may never have had contact with previously.

How Can I Be an Effective HRD Manager When I Am Not an HRD Expert?

You and your organization must first recognize that you cannot (and probably should not) be expected to be an expert on HRD. Indeed, your assignment to the position may be based on your organization's policy that the head of the HRD function should be a line manager or somebody from another staff function. We could argue the advantages and limitations of this approach, but they will become apparent in other parts of this book. For now, we accept the reality that appointing a non-HRD person to head the HRD function is accepted practice in some organizations. Throughout the remainder of this book you will find a good deal of material that will help you in that assignment.

Training, Educating, and Developing: Different Activities for Different Results

The term *human resource development* covers a wide range of activities. If your organization tends to lump together all the activities with the word *development* in the title and call them HRD, do not be confused. In our view, it is not appropriate to include economic *development* or marketing *development* as part of HRD just because they contain a similar word. To restate the point made in Chapter One, HRD is the mechanism through which an organization provides learning to employees, essentially to deal with performance problems and to take advantage of job opportunities.

What Can the HRD Function Provide in My Organization?

The major activities of HRD are concerned with learning and with consulting. Both can be helpful to you as a manager. This chapter focuses on the different kinds of learning that can be provided through HRD, while Chapter Four will discuss the consulting possibilities that might be available through your HRD unit.

What Are the Different Learning Areas of HRD?

There are three HRD learning areas, each with its own focus and objectives: training, education, and development. Although we discussed them in the first chapter, we believe the distinction between them is important enough to restate here.

Training is the activity where the learning is focused on the *present job* of the learner. Education is the activity where the learning is focused on a *future job* for the learner. Development is the activity where the learning does *not* focus on a job. It is important for you to be able to distinguish clearly between these, for each has a different contribution to make when it comes to solving problems or taking advantage of opportunities. You will note this as you look at the questions and answers that follow.

Why Should I Provide Training?

There are various reasons you should provide and support training. Among the most common and obvious are to alleviate performance deficiencies, to help introduce new products and processes, and to disseminate new policies. These will be discussed below.

It is also important to realize that you can support training at many different levels. At the very least, you may make employees available to attend a training program. You may do much more, such as provide some or all of the training budget or assist in the design of training to ensure that it relates to the problem it is intended to solve. You may even be involved in evaluating the training when the learner returns to the job — under you.

How does HRD relate to dealing with performance deficiencies?
There can be many reasons for performance deficiencies. It may be that you have a new employee who had the required general competencies when hired but now needs training to be able to relate those skills to the needs of your particular unit. You may have employees who have performed well in the past but have begun to slip in their performance. This is frequently seen in the workplace, particularly among employees who have been on the job for a long time. They will tend to take shortcuts in procedures or operations. That is certainly not unusual and should even be expected. As long as there is no penalty of any kind, that behavior can be expected to continue, and the number and types of shortcuts will increase. Then one day, as the result of a shortcut, you are notified of a quality problem! The employee may have been doing the job using shortcuts for such

a long time that the appropriate job behavior has been forgotten. Training is one way of bringing performance up to the level that you want.

How can HRD assist me when new products or processes are introduced? A good employee can suddenly begin to perform badly, and you may not realize that it is due to the introduction of a new product or a difficult process. As a manager, you probably agreed with the research and development people on the new product. Perhaps the idea came out of the marketing unit, and it seemed that your unit would be required to make only minor changes to bring the new product on line. If you did not provide training, it is very possible that some of the processes required for this new product were not familiar to your work force. Without training, your employees learned the processes the hard way, by trial and error. That is a very costly way, with the ultimate price being much in excess of what proper training would have cost.

Can HRD be helpful to me when new policies are issued? The effects of new policies may be more difficult to identify than the effects of new products and processes, but the resultant difficulties may be similar to what was described in the preceding paragraph. For example, a new policy related to safety may not change anything until appropriate training is provided.

This kind of situation became apparent in the mid 1960s and early 1970s, when many companies adopted positive policies to hire minority group members. Unfortunately, this change of policy was seldom accompanied by a training program for the current employees, and then only when there was a crisis. That change in policy required training to make the policy work without disrupting the organization.

It should be noted that almost any change in policy affecting people may require training. If you are given new policies or find yourself in a group making new policies, always consider the people who will be affected. How might training be helpful in implementing that new policy?

Why Should I Provide Education?

Education is learning for a clearly defined future job, not merely learning for some general use. It can be valuable for coping with promotion, lateral transfers, organizational upswings and downturns, and career development.

You may consider that it is not fair for you to be asked to use your resources to educate employees who will then move on to another unit. This is a valid objection and one that is all too frequently ignored. When you are asked to use your resources, it may be necessary to point out that it might be more proper for some other part of the organization to fund education for your employees.

It is a different matter if your organization has a firm policy that it is the responsibility of managers to prepare people for other jobs and that every manager should build this into the departmental budget. In such a case, consider that somewhere else in your organization another manager is educating his or her employees to move into your department.

How can I use HRD education in planning for promotions? A common requirement of a manager is the preparation of people to be promoted. This preparation is the most frequent use of education, and education should accordingly be tied in closely to the human resource planning effort, as well as to the plans for specific promotion and/or replacement of people in the organization.

By providing education, the manager ensures that the appropriate work force will be available when needed. Sometimes this is done by providing education for new employees before they go on the job. Airlines, for example, have extensive education programs for new employees who will serve as cabin crew. These new crew members are not permitted to go on the job until they have successfully completed the airline's program, provided at a cabin crew education center. (In many airlines, this is still referred to as the training center.)

How can I use HRD education when planning for a lateral transfer? The response to this question depends in part on the reason for the lateral transfer. It may become necessary when management has decided on a change in a product line or in services to be performed that will result in a different organizational configuration. Employees may become redundant in their present units, but with appropriate education they can readily be reassigned to other units in the organization. Of course, sometimes managers use this redundancy as an opportunity to divest themselves of less-desirable employees. This can result in decreased employee morale, whereas a carefully designed education program might make those employees quite effective in new jobs.

Lateral transfers are also utilized when an employee is facing burnout from doing the same job or same kind of job for many years. Doing another job in the same organization can be helpful to a good employee, as well as useful to you. Through education, the employee has a chance to find out enough about the new job to determine if it is appropriate. It also provides you with some insight about the possibility of success for the employee on the new job.

My organization goes through periods of upswings and downturns. How does HRD relate to those movements? Change is a constant in almost all organizations. There are very few organizations that do not face periodic upswings and downturns, and there are many reasons for these changes. Some changes arise from internal factors, such as changes in leadership or in the management philosophy of existing managers. Other changes are the result of external forces such as the marketplace, government regulations, and the available work force. One of the challenges that face most managers is how to plan for those changes — some anticipated and some unanticipated. HRD can be helpful by providing the needed learning experience at the most appropriate time.

Let us examine the upswings and downturns separately.

How can HRD education help on the upswings? For most organizations, the upswings are looked forward to with great enthusiasm. They usually mean that things are going well; often they are related to expansion of some kind, such as the opening of new markets, facilities, or sites. One way for an organization to cope with this is to hire new people. Frequently, however, it is more beneficial to prepare some of your existing employees for the new jobs that will arise from those changes.

The upswing can provide for more promotional opportunities, as discussed above — or for lateral transfers. It can mean either slight changes in desired performance or massive changes. Through appropriate education, your people can be prepared to cope effectively with those changes and make the upswing a positive organizational and personal experience.

A unique aspect of the upswing is that it can produce more promotional opportunities than usually exist, but many of these may be in areas where jobs have not previously existed. It is possible to design educational learning experiences for new jobs, but this is more difficult than merely educating somebody for a job that has previously existed. The earlier your HRD people are involved in the upswing, the sooner you will get the qualified work force you need.

How can HRD education help on the downturns? Downturns are usually viewed as being negative and sometimes involve retrenchment or downsizing. They may arise as a result of a declining economy, and they frequently include a move to cut all expenses. It may seem cost-effective to reduce or eliminate education until the performance records are examined.

Downsizing may include retrenchment — shifting employees to lower-level jobs. Often, those employees do not function effectively on their new jobs even though they may be judged overqualified. Actually, it is quite likely that they needed *more* education to prepare them for those jobs.

Even if the downturn or downsizing is the result of factors other than the economy, employees and the organization can benefit from effective HRD education programs. In addition to the benefits to be gained from the program objectives, the very existence of these programs can help employees to feel that the organization is concerned about them. This is important during a downturn.

What is meant by downsizing? In general, downsizing means reducing the number of employees in the organization. It can arise from a variety of needs, perhaps the most common of which is the need to cut costs and operating expenses in an attempt to become more profitable. This is usually referred to as becoming "lean and mean," though it certainly is not necessary to become mean in order to be lean.

Related to this is the downsizing that occurs when an organization decides to eliminate satellite sites such as regional or district offices. This may be done because it is necessary to save money or because those locations are no longer suitable.

Another reason for downsizing can be that a decision has been made to discontinue a product line. This happens quite frequently in the automobile manufacturing business when a company decides to discontinue a particular kind of car. Similarly, a service organization can decide to discontinue a particular service it has been marketing.

We are downsizing; how can HRD help? It is unfortunate that HRD is often not considered when downsizing occurs. Despite the fact that HRD can make a positive contribution, it may even be reduced or eliminated. The decision depends, in part, on the reason that an organization takes such a step and on its policy regarding employees.

If the organization wants to reduce its total number of employees by downsizing, the question that arises is, what will the remaining employees be expected to do? It is possible that functions formerly performed by the displaced employees will have to be absorbed into the jobs of those who remain. In order to make downsizing successful, a massive training effort will be required *before* the actual downsizing takes place, so that the transition to the new organization can be effective and efficient.

Even when sites are closed, the organization may still want to retain some of the employees who had worked at those sites. They may need training to be able to handle the same job in a different location. They may need education if, as a result of the downsizing, some of the employees will soon have different jobs.

It is unfortunate that during downsizing some managers take the position that they cannot afford to provide either training or education. Some managers are afraid that if they send employees for training or education, it will send a signal higher up in the organization that they have too many employees. Otherwise, how could they spare some employees to be off the job for learning? Actually, just the reverse is true. By providing the appropriate training and education, the company can make the downsizing more efficient, and the employees who remain can be made to feel an integral part of the organization.

How does HRD education relate to career development? If your organization has a career development program, then it should also be providing education to implement the recommendations from that program. There are elements of career development that do not require any learning, but where learning will facilitate the implementation of a career development plan, there is a place for education. It is not helpful when a manager offers employees career development planning opportunities without providing some or all of the education required in order for a career development program to be successful!

Why Should I Provide HRD Development?

This question is a bit more difficult to answer because it relates to learning activities that are not job related. Most managers feel that they must focus only on those activities that relate to the job and that meet the mission and goals of the organization. Therefore, most managers can see the need for training and education but find it a bit more difficult to see why they should provide development — learning that is not job related.

One of the problems in encouraging a manager to provide development is that there are usually no rewards for the manager. Both training and education are geared to result in improved performance. Training in particular should be reflected in lower costs, increased output, or higher quality — depending upon the goal of the training program. It is much more difficult to see how development can contribute to making your unit perform better, so your hesitation to use development is understandable. The next few questions will address some of the possible benefits of providing development.

What is meant by learning readiness? Learning readiness means simply being ready to learn, and it is very apparent in preschool children. Not every child is ready to go to school at a given age, even though laws are passed as if all children were the same. Some are ready to learn, while others are not. If a preschooler holds a book in a reading position, turns the pages one at a time, and recognizes that they tell some kind of story that has a beginning and an end, that child is probably showing learning readiness.

How does learning readiness apply to the people in my organization? Learning readiness also exists in most adults, but it is not nearly so easy to recognize. The reverse — lack of learning readiness — can be observed, however, and you may have experienced it. Consider an adult who has had successful school experiences through college but then goes no further. If ten years later that adult is asked to go into a learning situation, he or she will frequently find reasons not to go, using various rationalizations and explanations about work load and other priorities. Often this is an expression of a lack of learning readiness. That adult has been away from a learning situation so long that it is frightening to consider returning to it. On the other hand, if that adult has been engaged in various learning experiences since graduating from school, the new assignment to a learning situation does not present any problems. That adult is learning ready.

Development is one way of creating learning-ready adults, employees who are ready to go into a training or education situation with no hesitation or fear. Through development (non-job-related learning), the employee is in a constant state of learning readiness. This can be an expensive process, so development must be carefully planned not to deplete the financial resources that must be available for other HRD programs.

How does development relate to unforeseen organizational changes? Although there is no hard evidence, it has been suggested that development can help prepare employees for the unforeseen organizational changes that are almost a constant in the workplace. People who are ready to learn are more apt to be sensitive to new forces and movements. One reason for this is that they will have been experiencing change during their development learning experiences. Consequently, they will not find it too difficult to cope with other new ideas and experiences.

There are those who suggest that some nonorganizational activities, such as Outward Bound or similar outdoor programs, can enable people to have less fear of the unknown. These programs are characterized by taking employees to external locations, usually a kind of wilderness. There, under careful supervision, they will presumably learn how to work together. Although solid research on this is lacking, it is certainly something for a manager to consider.

Can I use development to show that I care for my employees? Some managers provide development because they see it as one way of showing concern for the individual. Providing training and education may show that a manager is concerned with employees only in relation to the work situation. Through development, a manager can show concern for the individual that is not limited to the work situation.

There is no evidence, however, that such concern will result in improved morale or job satisfaction. Some managers like to think that it will, and it may. It is just that there is no research that shows this.

If you want to use HRD development for that purpose, it would be best to check with your employees to determine how they would view it. Some may be receptive to it, while others may see it as a nuisance that gets in the way of doing their jobs.

Why Should I Be Interested in Making Decisions About HRD?

If managers do not make decisions about HRD, others will make those decisions instead, and the managers will have to live with the results (or lack of them). Throughout this book there will be references to specific decisions, but at this point just a few of them will be discussed: namely, staffing, allocation of facilities and funding, evaluation, and placement of HRD in the organization.

What kinds of staffing decisions should I consider? You should be concerned about HRD staffing even when that function does not report to you. The purpose of the HRD function is to serve your unit, and if HRD does not have the right people (and enough of them), you may find you are not able to get the service you need.

What do I need to consider about facilities and funding for HRD? Resources in any organization are generally limited. In part, your decisions will influence how those resources are allocated for HRD in your organization. Of course, you want everything for your own unit that you think it needs, but it is also necessary to provide needed resources to the HRD unit itself. If your decisions on this are appropriate, the HRD unit can serve you very well and allow you to use your own resources more effectively.

Why should I be concerned about evaluating the HRD unit or any aspect of its work? If you utilize the HRD unit, you should be involved in the evaluation of its output — the possible changes in the behavior of your employees. You must decide, with the HRD unit, how and when that evaluation should take place. The HRD unit will probably want to involve you in the evaluation effort, and you must decide whether you want to be involved. Generally, your decision should be to become involved.

Where should HRD be placed in my organization? There is no one answer to this question that can possibly cover all organizations and situations. Throughout the book some of the different items you must consider will be discussed. If possible, you should be involved in the decision regarding placement of HRD. Of course, to contribute to that decision requires that you know enough about HRD to make an appropriate contribution. This book should help you in that decision-making situation.

Should We Have HRD Programs?

In a sense, this suggests that you have an alternative. In reality, this question should have only an affirmative response. If not, your organization will pay for the lack of HRD in a variety of ways. To put it another way: if you think HRD is costly, consider how expensive ignorance is. You may very well have difficulty in reaching your departmental goals if you lack employees with the necessary competencies that could be provided through HRD.

Some managers think they can save money by not providing HRD programs. Instead, they fill their needs by actively recruiting (pirating) from other employers. This, however, usually means spending more money on recruiting, benefits, and higher salaries to get those employees. Even so, at some future time those employees will need to know more to enable them to keep up their performance and be up-to-date where technical skills are involved. The opportunity to keep learning is precisely what HRD provides.

Who Should Attend HRD Programs?

Attendance at HRD programs should not be seen as either a reward or a punishment. You should carefully select those who are to attend. Your organization is providing the facilities and funding for HRD, and it is up to you to make the most effective use of those resources by selecting people for HRD programs who can benefit the organization and themselves. Of course, this also includes you.

How Much Should We Spend?

This is a frequently asked question to which there is no one specific answer. Some organizations approach this decision by allocating a percentage of payroll for HRD. This normally ranges from 1 to 5 percent. However, you should not arbitrarily fix on a percentage in this range or copy another organization. If you decide to go the percentage route, you will have to develop your own criteria to do that. These criteria will be influenced by your type of employees, changes in technology and the marketplace, the labor market supply, and your competition.

As will be seen later in this book, there are various ways to do HRD budget planning, and that should also be considered in deciding how much to spend. The bottom line is how much you will have to spend to provide the HRD you need to reach your objectives.

Should We Set Aside Special Space for HRD?

It rarely happens that all of HRD is provided outside the organization. It is even doubtful whether that is a sound approach. To provide HRD within the organization, it may be necessary to set aside some space. The location of the HRD unit, as well as the space it can use for instructional purposes, communicates a clear message to your employees about how much you value that activity. To hide it away or to locate it in what is generally considered an undesirable location can make your HRD unit much less effective, no matter what other resources you make available to it.

In recent years, some large companies have taken bold steps in creating what are termed corporate conference centers. Xerox, IBM, Motorola, and Pepsico are among the many companies that have built dedicated HRD facilities at what appears to be a great cost. They have recognized that the cost will be returned many times over because the facility will really pay for itself in providing the appropriate atmosphere to conduct learning.

Should Managers Be Instructors?

There are times when your HRD people will ask you to be an instructor. You may want to say no, feeling that the time it takes to develop competency as an instructor will take you away from your basic job as a manager. However, if your HRD unit is good, its staff will be able to help you develop that competency (if you want and need it) in a relatively short period of time. In exchange, you will get many benefits.

Knowing something about teaching will help you in giving instructions to your employees. You will also find that having that competency can be very helpful when you have to provide on-the-job training to your employees.

Your presence in the HRD classroom will be one way of communicating your support, as well as providing you with an opportunity to find out what the HRD unit is doing. It can also provide you with informal contacts with some employees that you might not normally get to meet. The benefits will far outweigh the extra effort on your part.

Is HRD Only for Employees?

For the most part, HRD is for employees, but there are situations where HRD can and should be provided for nonemployees. If, as a manager, you are responsible for franchisees, you should consider providing the necessary training and education for them. Your job as a manager might involve dealers or other people who are not employees of your company but who are closely related. The concept of "just in time" may also require that you provide some training for your suppliers so that they can perform up to your standards of quality and time.

There are other nonemployee situations that a manager can be involved in. Not all of them require HRD, but where they do, you must consider it as a regular management responsibility.

The HRD Staff: Who They Are and What to Expect from Them

Why Should I Be Concerned About Staffing HRD?

Most managers are involved in some areas of staffing but frequently do not see the need to be concerned about staffing the HRD unit. However, the way that unit is staffed and the kinds of people recruited or assigned to it is of concern to all the managers in the organization. If the HRD unit is to be of service to you, you need to know the kinds of people the unit should consist of and the people who actually fill those positions.

Do I Need to Be Concerned Even When the HRD Unit Does Not Report to Me?

At another point in this book there will be a discussion of centralized and decentralized placement of the HRD unit. It is important to note, however, that in a decentralized arrangement you may have an HRD unit reporting to you. In that case, of course, you would be very concerned about the staffing.

When the HRD unit is centralized or in a different part of the organization than your unit, it should still be of concern to you. When you call on it for service, you will want to have some idea of who in that unit can provide the service you need.

Is a Manager Ever Asked About Staffing HRD?

Unfortunately, the response to this question is probably "very seldom." Too many managers do not see the HRD unit as being of help to them in solving problems, even though that is the major reason for having an HRD unit in an organization.

They also do not understand how HRD can assist them in taking advantage of opportunities. In most situations, managers cannot see any sense in being involved with the staffing of a unit of the organization that seems irrelevant to them.

Most managers should be asked about staffing HRD, even though the final decision may be made by the HRD manager. As will be seen in the following questions, there are many staffing possibilities, and the decisions should reflect your needs as a line manager.

What If I Am Not Asked About HRD Staffing?

If you are not asked, it usually would not be out of line for you to suggest that you are interested—that you want to be asked. If this has not previously been done in your organization, you may be looked upon with some degree of suspicion. That is because few non-HRD managers ever get involved in staffing the HRD unit, though that involvement would be highly desirable.

To be effective in your responses about staffing, you need to know just what the HRD people can do. That is the focus of the next set of questions.

What Do HRD People Do?

There are a number of different ways of looking at what HRD people do. The model presented in this chapter was first researched in 1958. It presents a "roles" approach. Since then, a number of other research studies have resulted in minor modifications of this approach, but the essential roles remain the same. Of course, the way those roles are performed has changed due to the increased use of technology and changes in the makeup of the work force.

What Is a Role?

A role is what a person thinks he or she is, but only when he or she is seen the same way by others. For example, a person can be appointed a manager, but that person does not really have the *role* of a manager unless and until others in the organization see that person as a manager. It can be summed up in the statement: "It takes two hands to clap."

The HRD people may see themselves in various roles, but until the managers in the organization see them that way, the roles are not viable. Therefore, you have to know what the possible roles are and then decide whether you want to see your HRD people that way. Later we will discuss some of the specific things that HRD people do in those roles.

What Are the Roles of HRD People?

HRD people can be seen in three *major roles:* manager of HRD, learning specialist, and consultant. Within these three major roles there are several *sub-roles* that will be discussed below. The HRD people in your organization may not fill all these roles, but these are the possibilities that exist. If you know them, you can indicate the roles you want filled that will assist you in your work.

What Can I Expect of an HRD Manager?

As with any other manager, the HRD manager is responsible for some management activities, including delegating some of the sub-roles to others in the HRD unit. Your major expectation should be that the HRD manager will be like other managers in your organization — responsible for meeting goals and objectives with the resources that are available. In addition, the HRD manager has some specific sub-roles to play: supervisor of HRD programs, developer of HRD personnel, arranger of facilities and funding, and maintainer of interpersonal and interdepartmental relations.

What does the HRD manager do as a supervisor of HRD programs? In this sub-role, the HRD manager carries out many of the usual supervisory functions. He or she provides programs to meet your needs — to help you solve problems or take advantage of opportunities.

To do this, it is necessary for the HRD manager to find out what you need — what problems you have and how HRD can provide a solution. The HRD manager will also work with you in helping to select those employees who can benefit most from the HRD experience. You will want to know the results, too, so the HRD manager will work with you to evaluate the learning that took place in the program. After all, the final result — change in job performance — can only be accomplished with your help when the learner returns to the job. It is also the responsibility of the HRD manager to determine how the various HRD programs relate to overall organizational objectives.

Part of the supervisory responsibility of the HRD manager is to work with you on scheduling programs at times when they can meet your needs. The decision of when to offer a program rests with the HRD manager, so your input on scheduling is crucial. The HRD manager has some constraints, of course, but the focus should be on providing HRD programs when and where you need them.

The HRD manager will assign specific HRD personnel to a program, but there are times when you will be asked for your suggestions as to the best HRD person for a particular program. Like any other manager, the HRD manager will appraise the performance of his or her own personnel, but he or she may come to you for additional data as you are the customer who is being served by the HRD staff.

Should the HRD manager provide me with information about the attendance of my employees during an HRD program? The HRD manager should keep you informed of the attendance and participation of your employees in the program. When you send employees to an HRD program, you should make sure that those employees know that their major responsibility at that time will be to attend and participate, and you should expect to get specific information about that from the HRD unit.

This also means that when you send employees off the job to an HRD program, provision should be made for coverage so that they will not have to leave the HRD activity while it is in progress to return to the job. There can always be emergencies, but they should be kept to a minimum so that attendance and commitment to the HRD program are not compromised.

If you wish to use external HRD resources — that is, to

have external HRD people conduct programs in-house — or to send your employees to external locations, your HRD manager can be of help by identifying the HRD resources that are qualified to help you with a specific problem or opportunity.

What does the HRD manager do to develop HRD personnel? Just as you are responsible for the development of your people, the HRD manager is responsible as a developer of HRD personnel. For the most part, this will be an internal affair, with the HRD manager handling this function as part of the operation of the HRD unit. The major effort here, on the part of the HRD manager, is to produce the best in-house HRD staff possible.

What about my people who might have a temporary or part-time assignment to HRD activities? In addition to the regular HRD staff, there are others who will work closely with the HRD unit from time to time. For example, the HRD manager could call on you or your staff to work with the HRD unit on a specific project, perhaps as a subject matter specialist (also sometimes called subject matter expert) when the HRD unit needs expert input to design a learning program. Another common linkage is when you or your staff are called upon to teach all or part of an HRD program.

The assignment may be on a full- or part-time basis. You may make a member of a work unit available to the HRD unit for a limited number of hours, or you may assign that person to work full-time with the HRD unit for a given period.

In either situation, the HRD unit should provide some orientation and perhaps even some training. You should not view this as an attempt on the part of the HRD manager to pirate your staff. Rather, the objective of the HRD manager is to make line people as efficient as possible while they are working in or with the HRD unit. Therefore, it is the responsibility of the HRD manager to provide learning experiences for your people. You should view it as a plus, for your people will be returning to your unit with additional competencies that they did not have when they left.

Do I have any place in helping to develop HRD personnel? It can also happen that HRD personnel are assigned to you on a temporary or part-time basis. One reason for this might be to give the HRD people a feel for how your part of the organization functions. Your support for such an assignment is essential. It is more than just giving you a temporary or part-time hand to help you get your work done; rather, it is to improve the ability of the HRD people to provide the kind of HRD service you need.

Why should the HRD manager be concerned with facilities and funding? Every manager, in some fashion, is concerned with funding. Without a budget, little or nothing happens. There fore, the HRD manager's concern with funding is obvious. The term *facilities* includes such items as an instructional center, designated classrooms, storage facilities, and housing accommodations. These can be provided internally, as when organizations allocate or construct specific space for HRD activities. They can also be provided externally by renting space in hotels, motels, and conference centers.

The concern with facilities may not be so obvious until it is recognized that having adequate HRD facilities is essential to an effective HRD program. There are some line managers, such as those who manage an external sales force, who do not require much in the way of facilities. Most managers, however, do require some facilities, and for the HRD manager they are crucial.

The HRD manager should provide reports on how the facilities and funding are utilized. Some of this information is important to you, and it would be helpful if you could indicate to the HRD manager what kinds of information would help you make more informed decisions about HRD.

What does the HRD manager do in arranging for facilities? This is one of the sub-roles that is frequently delegated or assigned to other employees within the HRD unit. Through this sub-role, the HRD manager can arrange to make suitable facilities available to you for any HRD programs you want to conduct. This includes arranging for those available internally as well as seeking out external resources when needed. The HRD manager should be able to do this for you whether or not the program is actually conducted by the HRD unit.

Why should I be concerned about what the HRD manager does to obtain funding? In every organization, there are limits to the amount and availability of funding, but the HRD unit needs funds in order to function. These funds can come from various places, as will be discussed in Chapter Five. You do not need to be concerned with the internal allocation of HRD funds, since that is the responsibility of the HRD manager. However, when the funds come from other parts of the organization, including your own budget, you should be concerned and involved.

What does the HRD manager do in maintaining interpersonal relations? To accomplish the objectives of the HRD function, the HRD manager must maintain relations with various individuals and groups, both inside and outside your organization (obviously, this includes you). When doing this, your HRD manager should not be trying to sell you anything but should just be keeping in touch, getting some idea of your concerns and plans. The initiative for this should come from the HRD manager, but it also requires that you open some doors. For example, why not invite your HRD manager (or HRD representative) into some of your staff meetings? It may not be appropriate to have that person at every meeting, but there are some meetings where you and your staff will be discussing problems for which HRD could provide an appropriate response.

When was the last time you invited your HRD people to your workplace just to talk and visit together? The HRD manager should be making this kind of visit to keep in touch with the reality of what is going on in the organization. Through efforts such as these, the HRD people can be more effective and more helpful to you.

What Can I Expect from a Learning Specialist?

The HRD learning specialist is the person you probably see most often, as it is the learning specialist who usually conducts classes. That is certainly not all the learning specialist does, but that is what you are most likely to see. Therefore, let us take a look at some of the other work done by HRD learning specialists. This role has the following sub-roles: instructor (facilitator), designer of learning programs, and developer of instructional strategies and materials.

What does an HRD person do as an instructor? We will start with the instructor, not because this is the most important sub-role, but because it is probably the most familiar. Actually, this sub-role should be called the *facilitator,* for that is more descriptive of what is being done. The HRD person should be facilitating the learning by the learner. Unfortunately, there is a tendency to reject that term as being jargon. Rather than take the time to argue that point, let us just recognize that the activities in this sub-role are designed to help overcome obstacles to the learning that is expected to take place. It may be group or individual learning, though using groups tends to be more common. As more small organizations are evolving in the United States, we can expect to see more individual learning situations or smaller groups. The increasing use of technology (computers for example) in learning situations allows for effective individual learning.

Learning experiences exist on a continuum, from those where only human instructors are used to those where machines act as the sole instructors. The reality of most learning is that it usually takes place somewhere along that continuum, with a mixture of the human instructor and the machine.

What does an HRD person do as a designer of programs? This is the sub-role in which the HRD staff member actually designs the learning experience that is to take place. To do this, the HRD designer should be using current models for designing programs.

There are many such models. Although you are not expected
to be an expert in adult learning, the designer must be. You
should inquire of the designer, however, what models or concepts of adult learning are being used. (This will be discussed
further in Chapter Six.) You want to be sure that the designer
is reflecting your philosophy and understanding of how adults
learn.

Am I expected to work with the designer? Yes. The designer cannot, and should not, work alone, because that designer is really
working for you and for the other managers who will be served
by the program. If you do not take part in the design process
or delegate one of your staff to participate, do not be surprised
if the result bears little or no relation to your problem and your
unit. To get the most out of the design process, you have to
invest the resources — time and people. You, or a member of
your staff, should be asked to serve as a subject matter expert.
You know the problems of your unit and what performance is
expected. The designer should be able to produce the kind of
learning program that will result in the performance you want
from your people.

What does an HRD person do as developer of instructional strate-
gies and materials? The person who fills this sub-role produces
the software for the computer, the slides and overheads for the
projectors, and other kinds of learning materials. The developer might come to you for substance, such as what should be
included in an exercise or case study. When making a videotape, the designer might ask you to be involved so that the final
product will represent the reality of your work situation rather
than some external, artificial studio environment.

     You are not expected to have any competency in writing
computer programs, making slides, or producing other instructional strategies or materials. Despite this, the developer of instructional strategies and materials can use your help so that
what is produced is appropriate for the learning program and
for your employees.

Can I expect all instructional strategies and materials to be produced in-house? Given the constant changes and advances in technology, an organization may decide to procure some of its instructional material from outside sources rather than have it produced by internal people. In such cases, the instructional strategies person may function not as a developer but rather as a resource person who knows where the appropriate instructional strategies and materials can be obtained.

When staffing internally, your organization may have to invest in specialized equipment, such as that for making slides. If there is not sufficient volume, the unit cost can be excessive — and this can lead to a tendency to use slides for everything, whether helpful or not, in order to reduce the unit cost. This has to be watched carefully when most or all of the instructional strategies and materials are produced in-house.

What Can I Expect from a Consultant?

As the consultant role is different from the major roles discussed above, it is discussed in a separate chapter (see Chapter Four). However, it should not be seen as being either more or less important than the major roles previously discussed. It is just that the consultant role requires different questions and responses.

How Many People Should There Be in the HRD Unit?

For many years, organizations have been searching for the magic ratio of HRD personnel to other employees. So far, nobody has found it, and probably nobody ever will. There are just too many variables that have to be considered, so that the ratio becomes a matter of "it depends."

The sub-roles discussed above might all be handled by one person in an organization, or there might be several people in each sub-role, or there might be special units for each sub-role. For example, in large, multi-site organizations it is not uncommon to find that the designer of programs and the developer of instructional strategies are located at corporate headquarters. The instructors, however, might be located closer to the various sites.

Generally, when the instructors come from line units — that is, when they are employees to whom you have assigned that task — the HRD unit itself may have few or no instructors. In such a case, the HRD unit must be sure to have a sufficient number of qualified designers to produce the needed programs. In that situation, the designers should be able to produce designs that can be used by non-HRD people.

Are HRD People Professionals?

This can be a difficult question to answer as there is no general agreement on what constitutes a professional. There are those who contend that for there to be a profession, there must be an agreed-upon body of knowledge, a code of ethics, and an organization that is considered a professional society. HRD has some of these, but not enough to really be considered a profession.

The word *professional* has come into general use for a wide variety of occupations. For this discussion, let us say that a professional HRD person is one who identifies with HRD as a specific field of occupational activity. As with many professions today, this is not necessarily a lifelong commitment.

Are There Different Kinds of HRD People?

It has been possible, through research as well as observation, to identify three different kinds of HRD people. They are grouped in the following categories: professionally identified (Category I), organizationally identified (Category II), and collateral duties (Category III).

These categories are not unique to HRD. If you are part of a professional group (engineers, medical doctors, scientists), you can readily identify your category through the discussion that follows. That is because the categories are based on research done in a variety of fields.

Who Are Professionally Identified
(Category I) HRD People?

Usually, it is safe to say that HRD people are professionally identified if they have been in the HRD field for at least five years and intend to stay there for the foreseeable future. Other identifying factors include the following: they hold membership in an HRD organization, they attend HRD meetings, they regularly read HRD publications, and/or they have done academic work in HRD. They may have come from outside your organization, having been recruited into an HRD position. They could also be people from within your organization who were temporarily assigned to HRD but then decided to stay and make it their career, in the process becoming Category I people.

Usually, Category I people are located in the HRD unit, but you could have some Category I people working directly for you in your unit. If so, it is important that you recognize their identification and support it. Some managers view HRD as being nonproductive and think that the goal of HRD people is to leave that activity and be assigned elsewhere. That is not the case if they are Category I, and you should not be recruiting Category I people for HRD with the intent of later moving them out of that function. Of course, some people may opt to do this, given sufficient incentives, but essentially the Category I person wants to remain in HRD.

Who Are Organizationally Identified
(Category II) People?

Generally, the average person found in an HRD unit is Category II, or organizationally identified. That is, these people have chosen to work for your company and will accept any assignment to any reasonable position. These people make up the bulk of any organization and can be found in all units and at all levels in your organization. Since most managers are Category II as defined here, you are probably one yourself. Sometimes even the HRD manager is in that category, which can present a problem if the people being supervised in the HRD unit consider themselves as Category I. This situation does not have to produce conflict, but frequently it does.

For example, some Category II people think that everybody in the managerial ranks of the organization should be in that category. This approach has some advantages, as it provides the organization with a group of experienced managers who are ready to move from one managerial position to another. It has the disadvantage that some units (such as HRD) may be staffed by managers who must try to learn a very complex operation in a short period of time. One result is that the HRD unit may become less effective for the organization than it would be otherwise.

Which Is Better for HRD, a Category I Manager or a Category II Manager?

There is no absolute answer to this question. The choice should be based on a careful consideration of the advantages and limitations of each kind of staffing.

An unnecessary conflict sometimes arises when a Category II person is placed in the position of HRD manager. It may signify to the HRD Category I people that there are few or no promotional opportunities available to them if they stay with the HRD unit in your company. It is also possible that a Category II HRD manager will have a short-range view of the HRD function. That is, that manager will want to make the best showing possible during the assigned time as an HRD manager. The Category I manager will be more concerned with the long-range goals of the HRD unit, goals that may go far beyond the short-term vision of a Category II manager in charge of HRD.

If you are assigned to be the manager of the HRD unit, those factors should be kept in mind. Despite those limitations, it is quite possible to have a very positive experience as an HRD manager. It can also add to your general background as a manager and give you some firsthand knowledge of how HRD can be a valuable resource to a manager.

What Is an Example of What a Category II Manager Can Do to the HRD Function and the Organization?

A general manager (Category II) was appointed as the HRD manager at the corporate level in a major automobile manufacturing company. He called his staff together and announced, "I am now the HRD manager and expect to be in this position for two years, since that is the general pattern. During those two years I want to make the best impression possible, for this could be a steppingstone to my becoming a vice president. I want to look good, and you are going to help in making me look good. Therefore, from now on we will devote our HRD resources to providing programs for managers and executives, so that they will know me and see how well I can manage." In fact, he wiped out almost all the technical HRD programs, which are essential to a manufacturing operation.

Fortunately for the company, the results of his decision became obvious after a few months, before too much damage had been done. The only real cost was to him; he was fired! He had turned an excellent growth opportunity into a loss for the company and himself.

What Is the Time Limit for a Category II Person to Be Assigned to the HRD Unit?

Category II people are assigned to the HRD unit under two different time parameters: time-definite and time-definite. Although it would be helpful if organizations would specify these time factors, our experience has shown that this is rarely done. Rather, it becomes an organizational culture factor and is expected to be understood; that is, "everybody knows" the time parameters.

However, we feel that the distinction is too important to remain unstated. Organizations should state these parameters explicitly even though they may change.

What does "time-definite" mean for a Category II HRD person? By time-definite it is generally understood that a Category II person will remain in the HRD unit for a given time, usually two or three years. It is rare for a Category II person to be assigned to manage the HRD unit for longer than this. Indeed, it sometimes appears that when a Category II manager is left longer in the HRD unit, it is a message that the individual cannot expect further advancement in the company.

On a more positive note, a Category II HRD manager can exhibit skill and competency that is visible to the entire organization, since the HRD unit can serve so many different parts of the organization. More than most staff functions, HRD must be involved in every aspect of an organization and at every level. If you, as a Category II person, are assigned to manage HRD, you should take advantage of the opportunity. It enables you to be in contact with many different people in the organization and to become personally familiar with what goes on in many different units.

What does "time-indefinite" mean for a Category II HRD person? When it comes to a time-indefinite assignment, there is no general agreement about how long the Category II manager will remain in the HRD unit. Time-indefinite assignments appear to be most common when an outstanding salesperson is made the HRD manager. There appears to be a tacit understanding that if that person is successful, the next step will be to a sales management position. However, there usually does not appear to be any specific time frame for that next step.

Who Are Considered As Having HRD Collateral Duties (Category III)?

Category III people do not actually move into the HRD unit. Rather, they stay in their regular units but are involved in some HRD programs. For example, the safety manager might conduct training programs on safety without ever going through the HRD unit. Of course, the familiar on-the-job training is a good example of this. You might even be doing that yourself, in which case you are a Category III manager. The reason for even discussing this category here is that if you are a Category III manager, you can still use some of the resources of the HRD unit even if you never leave your own workplace.

Should I Assign Any of My Own Staff to the HRD Unit?

In addition to the possibility that a manager like you may be assigned to manage the HRD unit, there are times when, as a line manager, you will be asked to assign some of your own people to work with the HRD people. Your people will be in the HRD unit for a short-term or temporary assignment — perhaps as a subject matter specialist, for example, since the HRD Category I staff are generally not hired for their expertise in the operations of your organization. To be effective, the HRD people need your employees to work with them in designing the appropriate learning experiences.

What Are the Benefits to Me of Assigning
Any of My Staff to Work in the HRD Unit?

There may be times when the HRD people might ask you to provide instructors. It is not that they are short-staffed, but rather that there are many situations in which instruction provided by line personnel can be more effective than instruction provided by professional instructors. Although this may appear to be a direct benefit for the HRD unit, there are two benefits for you as a manager.

First, when your line people are doing the instructing, they will probably produce a more effective program than an instructor who has not been living with the subject matter or the problem. The learners cannot retreat into the safety of saying, "But that instructor has never been in the real world of our job." At times, your staff, as instructors, may even add to the session from their personal experiences working in the organization.

Second, some of your staff will acquire additional skills (as instructors) that you can use in the on-the-job training that is part of your job. They will, in essence, receive training to be instructors and then have the opportunity to use that skill in a real situation. There will be differences, of course, for when instructing for the HRD unit they will be using special materials prepared by the learning specialists in that unit. For on-the-job training, you generally use your own materials, though there is nothing to prevent you from calling on the HRD unit to assist you in developing those materials. Another difference is that the instructor you assigned to HRD will generally be working there with a group of perhaps twenty employees, whereas on-the-job training is usually done for a much smaller group. Despite those differences, the benefits to you still outweigh the losses.

What Do I Lose When I Assign Staff to the HRD Unit?

Mainly, you lose the productive capacity of an employee for a given period of time. When it is a short-term or part-time assignment, you can probably cover by reassigning some tasks, postponing some, and delegating others. For a long-term assignment, other alternatives should be considered in conjunction with your human resources people and, perhaps, the manager to whom you report.

There is always the possibility, of course, that your employee will not return to you after such an assignment. Having exhibited highly desirable performance, that employee may then be transferred or promoted to another unit of the organization. You should consider this a positive reflection on your managerial skills in developing people. You obviously selected the right person to be assigned to the HRD unit — a person with potential.

For How Long Will the HRD Unit Want My People?

You may be asked to send one of your employees to the HRD unit for a long period of time, as noted earlier. It could be for as long as two or three years. When that is the case, you should involve the manager to whom you report and help that person recognize that temporary measures will not suffice. A replacement will be needed, with the understanding that the replacement may be removed when your regular employee returns. Generally, it is important for your regular employee to have the security of knowing that the job is being held for his or her return.

That means that when making the assignment you should consider all the possibilities. There are managers who, when asked to assign one of their people to the HRD unit, choose the person they feel can most easily be replaced. Alternatively, they may see this as a great opportunity to lose an employee they have been trying to get rid of for a long time. The result is that the HRD unit gets a less-effective employee, and it may hamper the quality of services you can expect from the HRD unit. It can also reflect on you, as a manager, that you do not seem to know how to identify people with potential.

How Should the Salaries of HRD Staff Be Determined?

Each organization has its own way of setting salaries. If yours is one in which they are set behind the scenes, with no open discussion, then you can skip this question. If, however, managers are involved in setting salaries, then this question is important for you.

There has been an unfortunate tendency to consider HRD staff nonproductive. This is a relic from the time when the major portion of our work force was in smokestack industries and the important jobs were those that related to getting the product out. This has changed greatly, and there has been increasing recognition that all jobs in the organization can be considered productive, even when they are done behind the scenes. For example, where customer service is concerned, every single member of the organization makes some kind of contribution.

The salaries for HRD staff should be considered in the same light as the salaries for others in the organization. However, since HRD performs a unique function in the organization, it may be necessary to identify different criteria than those applied to production workers, customer service personnel, or computer programmers. Criteria must be established that are consistent with other activities in the organization, particularly in the human resource area.

As with any other occupational group, consideration must also be given to what HRD people are being paid in other organizations. This is not easy to determine, even when other organizations agree to share that data, for what an HRD person actually does will usually vary from one organization to another. It may be possible, however, to put together a picture by looking at the kinds of roles your HRD people are expected to fill, as described earlier in this chapter.

Internal and External HRD Consultants: How to Select and Use Them

In some of the previous chapters we have noted that there would be further material on the role of the HRD consultant—and here it is. One reason for giving this subject a special chapter is because the word *consultant* has come to be used for a wide variety of people and activities, and this has led to confusion. Therefore, it is necessary to spend some time defining and explaining the word so that you can be in a position to make informed decisions about HRD consultants and how to use them.

What Is a Consultant?

A consultant is a person who helps another person to identify, to think through, or to solve a problem. The important word here is *helps,* since helping is the main thing a consultant does. A person should not be considered a consultant just because he or she comes from *outside* the organization, which is one of the common misuses of the term. As you will see later in this chapter, it is possible to have internal consultants—those who work in your own organization as consultants. It is not where the person comes from that makes it consulting, but rather what he or she does for you or with you.

What Are Some of the Reasons
I Would Want a Consultant?

There are many times when a manager needs help. You may be asked to do something for which you lack the competency and for which nobody in your unit has the competency either. For example, you may be asked to train some of your employees

48

to deal with a diverse work force. If you have never done that before, you would want some help from outside your unit, and the person to start with would be a consultant, someone who could help you to identify and understand the challenge of that particular kind of training.

Where Would I Look for a Consultant?

Generally, you should look for help from somebody outside the organization, or at least from someone who is not in your part of the organization. The reason for this is that you will want assistance from an objective source; that is, someone who cannot possibly be part of the problem or the situation. You are counting on the consultant to enter the situation with a detached point of view.

What Can a Consultant Decide for Me?

The answer to this is, nothing. You can use a consultant to help you make a decision, but the final decision must be yours. You are the one who will have to live with the results of that decision, whether good or bad. It must be your decision. There should be no hesitation about asking the consultant for help, but that should be kept separate from the actual decisions that have to be made.

Who Is Involved in a Consulting Experience?

There are always at least two parties involved in a consultation. They are the *consultant* and the *client,* who seeks help from the consultant. You may not want to be called a client, and some other word may be agreed upon (customer, for example), but you will find that generally you would be referred to as the client. Usually, consulting involves more than just a single manager. You will be part of a group called the *client system,* which may be just one unit of your organization or your total organization.

In some situations, there may be several consultants working together. For the purposes of this discussion, the term *consultant* will include situations where there are multiple consultants.

What Do HRD Consultants Do?

HRD consultants work in a variety of areas, and the ones described here represent only a small sample of the wide range of possibilities. For example, you will find an HRD consultant very helpful when you plan to introduce a new process. Even though things may be going along very well in your unit, a new process may be required because of new materials, new machinery, or a change in government regulations. Any or all of these may require a different kind of performance from your people than in the past, and the HRD consultant can help you to look at the changes and suggest those areas where training or education might be helpful.

To take another example, you may suddenly encounter a new kind of worker, different from those you have had before. This happened very frequently after 1964, when equal employment opportunity legislation was enacted to facilitate minorities entering the work force. A consultant who has experience with those programs can identify the potential problems and the kinds of learning experiences that would be helpful to various groups in your organization. In more recent years, managers have utilized HRD consultants for similar problems involving women, immigrants, and non-English-speaking workers.

What Should I Think About
Before I Consider Using a Consultant?

Being a client is not always easy and will almost always be a learning experience for you. Therefore, you must examine what you have to do as a client before becoming involved in a client-consultant relationship. There are no absolutes, as each relationship can be expected to be somewhat different. You and the consultant should have clear expectations of each other.

What Is My Relationship to the Consultant?

There must be a direct relationship between you (the client) and the consultant. It usually starts when the client invites the consultant to consider an assignment that could evolve into a relationship. Of course, the consultant must also agree to work for you in order for the relationship to start.

The relationship should be as open as possible, with both you and the consultant sharing all that needs to be shared to make the consulting assignment successful. If you should find that you do not trust the consultant or are uncomfortable in some way, it is best to terminate the relationship before it goes any further.

We have also seen relationships where the client and the consultant become so closely related that it becomes difficult to tell them apart. Closeness may be helpful, but when you feel that you are losing your managerial identity, it is time to look more closely at the relationship.

What Should I Expect of the Consultant?

You both have expectations of what will result from the client-consultant relationship. You and the consultant enter into that relationship for your mutual benefit. You, as the client, expect to get a service, usually in the form of a recommendation or a report. There may be some action taken, but only after you have made a decision based on the consultant's recommendation. You should not expect the consultant to implement the recommended action, because that is your responsibility as a manager.

You obviously expect your consultant to have competencies related to consulting. Sometimes this can be determined by having the consultant tell you about consulting work done with other clients. This will also help you find out if that consultant is ethical and respects client confidentiality (does not share company secrets or slander a former client).

What Should the Consultant Expect of Me?

The consultant expects you to participate and cooperate during the whole consulting assignment. A consultant is not meant to be used as an additional employee, just to get the work done. You have to be sure that you really want a consultant, not another manager or supervisor to whom you can delegate tasks. That is not what consultants should do.

The consultant expects to get paid or to receive some other agreed-upon recognition. An internal consultant, one from your own organization (but from outside your unit), may get paid from the budget of the HRD unit. It is also possible to have the services of the consultant charged back to your unit, depending upon the accounting policy in your organization.

What Should I Be Doing
During the Consulting Process?

The most important thing you can do is to be sure the consultant is working for you, not the other way around! Some managers get so tied up in the work of the consultant that they begin to look to that consultant for direction rather than advice.

You should, however, be constantly aware of what the consultant is doing. Too often, a manager hires a consultant (or gets one assigned from inside the organization) and then says, "OK, I have a problem. Now you take a look at it and come back next week with a solution. Meanwhile, do not bother me. I have other work to do. If I had the time, I could solve the problem myself." Careful — *you* might be the problem! Using a consultant will not give you more time. On the contrary, it usually requires that you allocate time to spend with the consultant.

The consultant must not make decisions — that is your job. When you use a consultant, you have to be prepared to spend time, as well as other resources, to make that consulting relationship a successful one.

When Does Consulting Start?

Although the relationship should always have a defined end, sometimes it has an undefined beginning. The consulting relationship can start in a wide variety of ways. You may be discussing a problem with somebody during a meeting, or even at a social occasion, when you discover that that person is a consultant and can help you. There may also be times when your boss suggests that you consider using a consultant, and so you meet with one or two just to explore whether you want to use them.

Even if you should decide to find a consultant on your own, there is still an exploratory phase when you will be interviewing several consultants. It is often difficult to determine exactly when the relationship begins. It is not even possible to say that it begins when the relationship is "on the clock" (being billed), for the relationship will usually start before any billing has been agreed upon.

When Does Consulting End?

There must be a clearly defined end to consulting. Both parties should have no confusion about when the present relationship comes to a conclusion. That does not mean that you and the consultant cannot proceed to another consulting relationship, dealing with another problem or need. This can happen even before the first relationship is concluded.

Coming to an unambiguous end is sometimes accomplished by a ritual or similar event that signifies to all concerned that this particular consulting relationship has now reached its conclusion. It may not be a satisfactory conclusion, but there should be no doubt in anybody's mind that the end has arrived.

What Kind of Ritual Might Signify the Conclusion of Consulting?

There are many possibilities, but it is important that your choice reflect the culture of your organization and leave no ambiguity as to its purpose. A common ritual is a drink over submission of the final report or acceptance of the final check. Not all celebrations involve food or drink; sometimes all that is required is a small ceremony. It is likely to go more smoothly if you plan it rather than just hope it will happen spontaneously at the end of the relationship.

What Do I Need to Know and Do to Be an Effective Client?

At the outset, you need to know what you are looking for and what type of help you expect from the consultant. Recognize, however, that as the relationship begins to develop, this can change. If a change does occur, you should be aware of when it happens and in what direction you and the consultant are going.

You need to know something about consulting models — at least to know that models exist. You should ask your consultant what model is being used. Most consultants have models for consulting, though they may call them guidelines, road maps, checklists, or something similar. If your consultant cannot produce some kind of model, you should be extremely cautious. You do not need a consultant who flies by the seat of the pants, making it all up as the situation develops. It is not necessary that the consultant stick strictly to the model if the situation appears to require something else, but at least you will know what you are deviating from.

You have to know how to share, to be open and forthright with your consultant. Too often, for various reasons, managers do not share all the necessary information with their consultants. Consequently, a major complaint of consultants is that their clients expect them to work miracles on the basis of inadequate information. If you are not prepared to share openly with your consultant, perhaps you are not ready to use one.

It can be expected that your previous experiences with consultants will color your relations with a current one, and that can lead to difficulties. Obviously, not all consultants are the same, and even the same consultant may function differently, depending on the nature of the problem or the type of consulting you are seeking.

Are There Different Kinds of Consultants?

You have to recognize that there are many different kinds of consultants, and unfortunately there are very few limits on who can call themselves a consultant. There have been various attempts to establish some kind of certification, but that has proven to be extremely difficult — virtually impossible. One reason for this is that consulting is an activity that covers many quite different fields: engineering, politics, organizational behavior, and so on.

Some people have found that they can make more money (charge more for their services) if they call themselves consultants rather than vendors or suppliers. You, as a manager, when considering the use of a consultant, should be less concerned with the title than with what that person (or company) can do for you.

Generally, however, consultants can be divided into two broad types: content consultants and process consultants.

What is a content consultant? The content consultant is one whom you call upon for the content of HRD — adult learning and the technology of learning. To take an example discussed earlier, let us consider how you could use a consultant if you planned to purchase new machinery. During the purchasing process you would undoubtedly involve your design engineers, your financial people, and perhaps your production managers. You should also involve your HRD staff as consultants to consider what, if any, learning programs will be needed to prepare your work force for the new machinery. At that point, you are not asking for a specific training or education program; rather, you are asking your HRD consultants to advise you whether such programs might be necessary and how they would relate to start-up time and full production on the new machinery.

What is a process consultant? A process consultant is what you would want if you were seeking help in thinking through a problem. For many years, the process consultant was utilized more frequently than the content consultant. One reason for this was that the process consultant could produce more dynamic changes in an organization. In addition, there were some good books written on how to be a process consultant, and those books got both clients and consultants interested in process consultation.

To take just one example, you might use an HRD process consultant if you were faced with the problem of getting your supervisors to work effectively with people from minority or ethnic groups they have not worked with previously. In this case, you would not be looking for solutions, at least not at the start. You would want to explore, with the help of a consultant, some of the things that might be done, how your supervisors might react, how a learning program could be put in place, how the supervisors should be involved, and so on.

How Does an HRD Unit Provide Consultation?

There are many ways to answer this question, but let us use a model that gives four ways an HRD consultant can serve you: as expert, as advocate, as stimulator, and as change agent. The first two are roles for a *content* consultant, the latter two for a *process* consultant.

How would I use an HRD consultant as an expert? You would want to call on the consultant as an expert if you thought that HRD might be a solution for a problem but you needed to know more about HRD in order to make an informed decision. The expert should be able to share with you his or her knowledge and experience of the HRD field so that you could make an informed decision.

For example, let us assume that you are planning to change your operation from one centered on individual performance to one centered on autonomous work groups. You know that this requires a much different kind of performance from your employees than they have produced in the past. You suspect that more will be needed than just providing them with training for new skills, but you are not sure what is involved or whether HRD has any part to play in this process. You call on your HRD consultant expert to help you identify the problems and to share with you what is known in the field about preparing employees to become part of an autonomous work group.

How would I use an HRD consultant as an advocate? In this case, you would call upon your HRD consultant to suggest specific responses to an HRD problem. In other words, you call upon the advocate when you feel you know the problem and are looking for possible solutions. You must still make the decision, but you are looking to the HRD consultant advocate to provide you with specific alternatives you can draw upon to make your decision.

For example, say you have decided to purchase a new piece of equipment that will require a different performance from some of your operators. Your supplier may or may not have agreed to provide the necessary training. You would feel more confident, however, if your own HRD consultant advocate could tell you the specific kinds of training that will be required and the advantages and limitations of each.

How would I use an HRD consultant as a stimulator? You would seek the stimulator as your HRD consultant when you felt the need for an alter ego—that is, someone to stimulate you to ask the questions about an issue that you yourself might otherwise not ask. In this type of situation, the HRD consultant does not have to be a specialist in your area. As always, the decision is yours. What you are seeking from your HRD consultant is simply questions, and this may take several sessions and a considerable amount of time. You should use your consultant liberally to provoke questions. Do not become annoyed if some of the questions seem unanswerable. In this sub-role, you are not using your HRD consultant to answer questions or give advice; you are using him or her strictly to help you explore the questions—to stimulate you to keep probing into the situation.

For example, say a human resource manager is asked to implement an equal opportunity program. Recognizing that there could be HRD implications, the manager calls upon an HRD consultant stimulator. They spend several sessions together during which the consultant encourages the human resources manager to ask questions about HRD, equal employment, and learning experiences that might be helpful. When they part, the HRD consultant does nothing more, for it is now up to the manager to decide which questions should be explored and what the next steps will be.

How would I use an HRD consultant as a change agent? The change agent assists you in thinking through how change can be brought about in your organization, particularly where HRD is involved. At times, it is possible that the change agent will go beyond the area of HRD, since other elements of the organization may have to be involved. It is important to note the emphasis on "agent," for bringing about change is something *you* should be doing as a manager. The HRD consultant should be assisting you — in effect, acting as a catalyst. In other words, the HRD consultant should be helpful in planning but should avoid becoming part of the change process.

For example, a manager may wish to change a series of working relationships. In essence, the manager should have already decided on what the new relationships should be. (If not, then the manager wants the HRD consultant stimulator.) Once the manager has decided on the change, the change agent can help the manager plan how to make the change take place, and the learning experiences will then facilitate that change.

What Is the Difference Between an Internal and an External Consultant?

The words *internal* and *external* have particular meanings in consulting, and it is important for you to know these in order to obtain the consultant who will meet your needs. Actually, there are *three* different possibilities — two meanings for internal and one for external. Internal can mean either a part of your operation (department, unit) or not a part of your operation but still a part of your organization. External means not in any way a part of your organization.

What is meant by an internal consultant who is a part of your operation? In this situation, the HRD consultant reports to you. It may not be direct, in that the HRD consultant may report to an HRD manager who then reports to you.

The general feeling about this situation is that you should be cautious about using that HRD unit except for certain kinds of consulting. There should be no problem when using that

HRD consultant in the content sub-roles (expert, advocate). There might be some realistic hesitation on your part in using your internal HRD consultant for process consultation (stimulator, change agent) when HRD is part of the problem. In this situation, you first have to consider whether your HRD consultant is part of the problem or will be involved in the solution. Before you make the decision on using this consultant, both you and the consultant need to be aware of the possible complications and conflicts.

What is meant by an internal consultant who is not a part of your operation? In this case, your organization has an internal HRD unit, with consultants available to you, but the HRD unit is located in another part of your organization. It might be an organization-wide HRD unit or just one that is in another part of your organization. The same factors must be considered as when the consultant is internal *and* part of your operation. Perhaps that is why many managers prefer to seek external consulting assistance (the next type discussed).

Of course, when the consultant is not part of your unit, there is less possibility that the consultant and the HRD unit will be part of either the problem or the solution. However, they still might be, and you have to carefully consider that possibility when determining what kind of consultant to use.

An advantage of using this type of consultant is that you get one who is familiar with your organization but not directly involved in your operations.

What is meant by an external consultant? This third possibility is fairly self-evident: the consultant is not currently employed in any part of your organization. Of course, that consultant may have worked for you previously, or for other managers in your organization, but he or she is not a regular employee of the organization. Even if the consultant is currently working with others in your organization, he or she is still not a regular employee.

The distinction that is frequently made between internal and external consultants is one of cost, but that should probably be the last factor considered. Indeed, if any external HRD consultant offers to work for little or nothing, be extremely careful, for that is what you will probably get — little or nothing. There may be some unusual circumstances when pro bono consulting is available, but they are very limited and must be looked upon with some suspicion.

One of the major benefits of the external consultant is that that individual can bring objectivity, new thinking, and insights to you. Presumably, if you have chosen carefully, that consultant has experience in a wide variety of organizations and situations that can be helpful to you in solving your current problem.

How Do I Find Internal Consultants?

If you are looking for an internal consultant, your HRD manager should be the primary source. Of course, you will also want to talk to other managers in your organization who have used the internal consulting services of your organization.

Many HRD units have consultants as part of the regular staff. Indeed, some have whole units of consultants. In Chapter Three, it was pointed out that you should be involved in staffing HRD to be sure that your HRD unit has the kinds of people you will need. If you have not previously encouraged HRD to have consultants on its staff, you should not be surprised when the HRD unit cannot meet your needs.

If your HRD unit (no matter where located) has consultants, you should carefully screen and interview them to be sure you are getting the kind of consultant (content or process) you are looking for. It is also a good idea to speak to other managers who have used the internal HRD consultants to see what their experiences have been.

Where Can I Find External Consultants?

The answer to this question is very simple — everywhere. As a manager, you are probably constantly being bombarded by flyers, leaflets, and other printed material from individuals and organizations offering you consulting services. You may even receive telephone calls or visits. Your boss may have had a good experience with a consultant or heard of a good one, and you may have been encouraged to use that consultant. Oftentimes, in these situations, you are being asked to use a consultant for a problem you did not know you had until you hired the consultant.

When Do I Decide Whether I Need a Content or a Process Consultant?

Once you have decided you need a consultant, you should consider which kind — process or content. If you are experienced in using consultants, you might be able to make this determination before you even look for the consultant. If not, you may just have to start with a consultant and then make that determination. This may mean that you will have to switch to another consultant, so be prepared for that.

Process consultants tend to be more available, and there seem to be many more of them, so you may have to do some exploring and interviewing in order to select the person or organization you think would be most helpful. Some consultants specialize in a particular kind of process consultation, while others use different models. The variations are so great we cannot possibly list them all here. Suffice it to say that you should not hesitate to ask questions. The process consultant may use some words you do not understand, and it is perfectly acceptable, even necessary, that you ask the consultant to explain. Do not let your ego get in the way; do not feel that asking questions makes you look dumb. After all, if that consultant were trying to understand your job and organization, he or she would undoubtedly have to ask questions about some of the terms you use.

When the consultation relates to content, it is sometimes easier to identify and understand the consultant. The terminology tends to be more readily understandable, and you are generally dealing with areas you know a bit more about. Even here, however, do not hesitate to ask questions to make sure the consultant has experience and expertise in the area you are concerned with.

Even in those cases where you are looking for an external consultant, your HRD manager can be helpful, but remember that the final selection decision should still be yours. If you do not have an HRD manager, or if you prefer not to consult him or her, it is still possible for you to locate external consultants on your own by contacting peers in other organizations, university faculty members, and so on.

Do External Consultants Work Individually or in Groups?

Both patterns are observed among consultants. Some prefer to work as individuals, while others seek to consult with a peer group of other consultants available to them. One is not necessarily better than the other.

What Should I Consider When Looking for an Individual Consultant?

For the purposes of this discussion, an individual consultant is a person working alone. Such a person might be less costly than a large organization, as there would be less overhead. However, if this person has an outstanding reputation and is in constant demand, he or she may be more expensive.

When considering the single individual, be aware that few individuals can serve in all the different sub-roles (expert, advocate, stimulator, and change agent). As an expert or advocate, for example, a single individual is unlikely to know everything about the particular field. This limitation is sometimes compensated for in a variety of ways that can be helpful to you, but you should ask the consultant about them.

Does an Individual Consultant Ever Involve Other Consultants?

It is not at all uncommon for consultants to work with each other. There are consultants who always work together on assignments (sometimes these are spouse teams), and there are a variety of other combinations as well.

A common practice, for the individual consultant, is to

utilize a shadow consultant — someone your consultant can turn to for advice, or just to have another party available while exploring options or techniques. Usually, you will not be in contact with that shadow — you may not even know the shadow exists. If you do discover that your consultant uses a shadow, it does not mean that your consultant is inadequate.

When Consultants Work Together, What Kind of Organization Do They Have?

You may prefer to deal with a larger group of consultants, and they are usually grouped in some kind of organization. "Some kind" may sound vague, but that is the reality of the field. There are organizations that do only consulting, while others may also provide learning programs or design learning programs for you. There are others that develop packaged programs in addition to providing consulting services. It is even possible to find organizations in another work area (accounting, for example) that also provide consulting services in HRD. However, there is one thing you can be sure of: having "consulting" in the title of the organization does not mean its staff members are consultants, and the absence of that word does not mean staff members do not serve as consultants. In other words, you should not base your exploration on organization titles but on solid descriptions of what staff members have done or think they can do.

What Should I Think About When Planning to Use an Organization of Consultants?

One consideration relates to the size of the organization and the types of work it actually does. For example, by using an organization, you could have a larger pool of consultants available to you than if you were dealing with just one or two individual consultants.

A consultant, working alone, may be tempted to keep you locked into the kinds of things that he or she can do. That is, of course, unethical, but in the absence of any way of policing consultant practices, you are the one who must be on the alert. An ethical consultant, in that situation, would refer you to another consultant who could meet your new need. When working with an organization, this can easily be accomplished by having an appropriate consultant assigned to you if you started with the wrong one or if the situation changes.

If I Use a Consultant from an Organization, How Can I Be Sure That the Consultant Will Stay with Me for the Whole Assignment?

You cannot be sure, and that is one of the limitations of using a consulting organization rather than an individual. Because an organization usually has many clients at the same time — many more than the individual consultant has — the managers in that organization may be prone to shifting consultants around to match the staffing needs of the organization. The organization may want to assign you a staff member who is not occupied at the time — and that might not be what you need. Sometimes this can be handled by appropriate wording in the consulting agreement (that is, if the agreement is actually put on paper). In other words, you must use your own judgment about accepting a different consultant to work with.

I Have Heard That Some Universities Provide Consultants. Is That Something I Should Consider?

The answer here is that it depends on the particular university. There is a wide range of policies that universities can adopt, and you need to consider these when looking to a university for consulting help.

Some universities do not allow their faculties to do any outside work. They can still provide consulting help, but it will be as field experience for their students under the guidance of a professor. The cost should be nonexistent or nominal, and you might still get some good consulting help.

Are Regular Faculty Involved in Consulting Outside the University?

Some universities allow faculty to do outside work for remuneration, with some limits. One such limit may be time; for example, the faculty member may only be able to work one day a week outside the university. Another is money; the faculty member may be allowed to earn only a certain amount from outside work (usually a percentage of his or her salary).

If I Choose to Use a Faculty Member, Am I Then Making a Decision to Use an Individual?

Not all faculty members work as individuals. In some universities they are allowed to form regular companies and provide consulting services. Such companies may actually use the name of the university, while in other cases they may be prohibited from using the university name in their title even though they are a unit of the university.

As with the organizations described previously, these companies have the strength of having a range of individuals available. Faculty members who work as HRD consultants come from a variety of university departments. One reason for this is that not too many universities have separate HRD departments, although the number is growing. However, you should be aware that there are many people who consider themselves knowledgeable about HRD even though they are not.

The content consultants will usually be found in departments such as business, engineering, accounting, and public administration. Process consultants will probably be located in departments such as education, counseling, psychology, and management science.

Considering All the Factors Involved, Do I Really Gain Anything by Using a Consultant?

You can answer this question for yourself. Look back through this chapter, for we have tried to point out the advantages and limitations of using a consultant.

If you have an urgent need and feel you cannot cope alone, by all means obtain a consultant. On the other hand, if you have any doubts, you are probably better off not getting involved with a consultant. It is, at best, a time-consuming relationship with ambiguous results. When you use a learning specialist, you should know from the beginning what the anticipated results are. In a consulting relationship, very seldom is it possible to foretell the results, even though the ultimate benefits to you may be great.

Providing Funding, Facilities, and Equipment for HRD

Where Does the HRD Unit Get Its Funding?

There is no one answer to this question, as it depends on the particular organization and how it is organized for financial purposes. It also depends on where the HRD function is located — that is, whether it is centralized or decentralized.

How does it work where there is a centralized HRD unit? If there is a centralized HRD unit — usually at some upper level of the organization — then that unit might obtain funding in the same way any similar unit does at that level. As you will see from the discussion that follows, there are various alternatives to this, and even a centralized unit might want to consider some options other than the system that currently exists.

How does it work where there is a decentralized HRD unit? A decentralized HRD unit located within an operational or line department might be financed in the same way as other activities within that department. No matter where it is located, however, there are several financing options, within the limits of the organization's policies.

What Is the Financial Center Concept, As Applied to HRD?

One way to look at funding the HRD function is through the concept of centers. This concept is not new, but unfortunately it is very infrequently applied to HRD. This is surprising, since the center concept has much to offer in making HRD as responsive as possible to managers' needs, as well as in providing essential data on what HRD costs.

Using the center concept, the HRD unit can be organized as a budget-item center, a cost center, a profit center, or some combination of these. With a budget-item center, the organization provides a budget allocation to the HRD unit. With a cost center, the HRD unit charges other parts of the organization for its services and products with the intent of recovering its costs (breaking even). With a profit center, the HRD unit charges others (within the company and outside) for its services and products with the intent of making a profit.

How does HRD function as a budget-item center? The budget-item center still tends to be the most common method of funding HRD. This is done by providing an allocation for HRD in the organization's annual budget. Naturally, this allocation should be based on the current and anticipated needs for HRD programs and activities. Generally, you and other managers only see the end result of the extensive work that your HRD people had to do when developing a program — a series of learning activities or a way of providing consulting.

The most important point here is that the cost does *not* come out of your (the line manager's) budget. Naturally, you will probably bear some indirect cost, as with similar services, since all the units of your organization are probably charged to cover company-wide costs.

Using a budget-item center, the HRD manager usually sends out a list of the courses to be offered, and line managers are encouraged to send their people to the appropriate programs. These will be general programs such as orientation, supervisory training, or supervisory education. These programs are predictable, as there is always the need for them. Control can be exercised over who registers, since the HRD unit can require that a registration form be countersigned by the employee's supervisor. Using your HRD unit this way does not, however, incur any actual cost on your part.

With this approach, the HRD unit will want to list as many different courses as possible. In some organizations one can find a thick book, much like a university catalogue, listing all the available courses. The offerings are usually planned well in advance and are marketed through bulletin boards, house organs, and memos. This is where you will see your HRD manager selling HRD offerings in order to get enough people to fill up a program.

There are some benefits to a budget-item center. It is relatively easy to keep track of specific and actual charges, so that the organization can obtain a very good idea of just what it is spending on HRD. It also means that the executives in the organization can be sure that HRD is being provided.

As can be expected, however, there are also drawbacks. The programs must be planned far enough in advance to allow for mass registration. It is possible that the employees who originally registered no longer need the learning experience when the program is finally offered, but despite that there is still pressure on you to send somebody to the program. This certainly is not cost-effective and contributes to the idea that the HRD operation does not serve the goals of your organization.

With a budget-item center, there is the tendency for the HRD manager to offer those programs for which there will be sufficient registrations to make them cost-effective. There is less possibility that the HRD unit will respond to immediate and specialized needs. Although there is nothing to prevent the HRD manager from setting aside some funds to cover unforeseen needs, in practice that rarely happens.

Another factor in running a budget-item center is the need to use the entire amount budgeted. In essence, the HRD manager risks being criticized if the HRD funds are not fully used during the budget period. The implication, of course, is that the unspent budget is the result of poor budgetary planning. This puts great pressure on the HRD manager to spend it all, regardless of whether there is a real need. One practice is to use the money to purchase unneeded equipment for HRD—at least then the HRD manager will have something to show for the money.

How does HRD function as a cost center? When looking at HRD as a cost center, it is first necessary to define what is meant by cost. Each organization will have its own criteria, but what is generally meant is that the HRD unit has to recover its costs by charging other units. Initially, the HRD unit gets little or no funding for the fiscal year. It is desirable, however, to provide some small amount in the HRD cost center budget to provide for general programs that would not be charged to departments, such as orientation of new employees.

Where, then, does the money come from for the HRD operation? The cost center is a reimbursable operation. That is, the HRD unit charges for its services. No actual money changes hands, but other units in the organization are charged through the appropriate accounting entry for the services they "buy" from the HRD unit.

The cost center approach can only work if you make a budgetary provision for HRD. If you, the line manager, do not allocate some budget for HRD, it will not be used. Of course, you cannot be sure during the budget preparation cycle exactly what you will need. As with some other budget items, you can only make a guess based on past experience and plans for the future.

An overriding factor in favor of the cost center is that the HRD unit must serve your needs — after all, if you do not use it, HRD will have no income against which to write off expenses. Through the cost center approach, the HRD unit must pay for itself.

There is another kind of cost, however, in the fact that an HRD unit organized as a cost center will tend to be very low risk and primarily reactive. The HRD manager will generally not want to try out new programs or risk offering programs that do not have a wide appeal. If you support having your organization's HRD effort as a cost center, do not expect HRD to respond to individual learning needs or to the needs of a small group of employees. For the HRD unit, that might not be cost-effective.

You can overcome that obstacle, in part, by providing the HRD unit with some limited funds for research and development and for specialized programs. HRD must still be accountable for those funds, but it will not be limited to developing programs for mass consumption.

If your HRD unit is located within your department, or if it reports to you, it is logical to examine the HRD unit profit-and-loss statement very carefully. This usually will not balance out at exactly zero — what manager could achieve that? You need to look at the profit side, if there is one, and determine the reason for the profit. Is HRD overcharging for its services, or has the HRD manager just been very successful in controlling costs? On the expense side, are the expenses logical ones that should be charged to HRD?

When there is a loss — and this can be expected — you should likewise look for the reasons. Was the loss due to poor budgeting or to unforeseen circumstances? Which specific activities contributed to that loss?

Even if you have no direct responsibility for the HRD function, you should still be asking those questions. After all, HRD is using the organization's financial resources. If it does not use them effectively, you will be paying for that in some way. If nothing else, it can mean that there are fewer resources available to you.

How does HRD function as a profit center? The profit center is much like the cost center in that it charges for its services, but there are some significant differences. For one, the profit center is generally allowed to market its products outside the organization. This situation arises under a variety of circumstances. It may happen when the organization realizes that the HRD unit has developed programs that are generic enough that there is an outside market for them. The original costs of development have generally been recovered, the programs have been used internally, and selling them externally will do no damage to the organization. Quite the contrary, it can enhance the image of the organization as well as bring in revenue. This path has been taken by organizations such as AT&T, General Motors, and Du Pont, among others.

Let us focus, however, on the internal profit center. Actually, this is not something that is very new. Back in 1940, when one of the authors worked for a company as an assistant manager in Department A (let us call it), he remembers being called on the carpet by the company president for charging back a product to Department B at a profit. The president wanted Department B to have a good financial statement, so he insisted that the internal charges to that department be at cost (no profit). Of course, this would be reflected adversely in the financial statement of Department A, which would be producing but not making a profit. It was a very important lesson on the need for clarifying just what a profit center is and how it should operate.

There are, of course, many organizations that do not use that internal charge system, and therefore the profit center concept would not make any sense. It is possible, however, to see a trend toward the profit center as one aspect of the "intrapreneurial" practice—making each department manager, in essence, the head of a miniature company.

Using the profit center approach can prove seductive because the HRD manager may discover that there is a larger market outside the organization than there is internally, and consequently efforts may get misdirected. The profit center approach also allows line managers to contract externally for their HRD needs, even to the extent of using competitors of their own organization's HRD unit. Even if the HRD profit center does focus its efforts internally, the tendency would be to stick to those programs that have the best rate of return, which may not be the programs for which there is the greatest internal need.

Can the HRD Unit Consist of All Three Types of Centers?

It is possible for an HRD unit to include all three types of centers, but that is very difficult to administer. If you are a line manager assigned to be the HRD manager, you should determine what past practices have been and then decide if they are still pertinent to your objectives.

As a line manager using the HRD unit in your organization, you need to know what to expect. For example, if there is a budget-item center, whose budget will provide for HRD expenses? They might come out of the corporate budget, or you might be expected to have HRD money in your own budget.

If the HRD unit is a cost center, whoever you report to may expect you to have HRD money in your budget. In that case, you will want to know what the programs might cost you. You will also want to know if you can only purchase your HRD services from within the organization or if you are free to purchase from outside the organization.

Similarly, when an organization has an HRD profit center, you need to know if you are limited to purchasing HRD services internally. Some organizations allow line managers to purchase outside, particularly if you can get the same service at a lower cost. This puts your internal HRD unit in competition with all the external suppliers of HRD goods and services.

What Do I Need to Know About My Company's Financial Policies Regarding HRD?

The previous discussion has shown that there is a direct relationship between the kind of financial center the HRD unit has and who pays for it. There may also be some other financial policies you need to consider. These could relate to a limit on amounts paid for external HRD or to what approvals are necessary for that. Generally, when purchasing internally (through a cost center), there are few or no restrictions.

One of the most common ways HRD is purchased externally is through the use of tuition reimbursement. The most usual form this takes is payment to a school, such as a college or university. It might also include organizations offering public seminars, such as the American Management Association. Limitations on these kinds of payments have varied from year to year under Section 127 of the Internal Revenue Code, so it is important that you consult with your HRD people before planning any program that would involve tuition reimbursement.

There may be some restrictions on the amounts or types of programs that are available to the different groups of employees in your organization. It is also possible that there are minimums that you are expected to spend on HRD within a fiscal year.

Should I Consider Buying a Packaged Program?

A packaged program is one that has been prepared by a supplier (vendor) who has the intent of selling it to a wide market. There are many organizations doing this, and your HRD people undoubtedly receive a great number of brochures in the mail about those programs.

As with almost any purchase you plan to make, there are advantages and limitations. The advantage of a packaged program is that you can get a learning program that is already developed and immediately available. Most of these programs are very professionally done. You have to decide whether you want to conduct the program yourself (or have one of your staff do it) or whether you want a program that will be a part of a total package including instruction provided by the supplier. Both are available. You will also hear the word *customize,* which means that the supplier is prepared to make some changes in the program to fit your particular needs.

There is nothing wrong with buying packaged programs. The chances are that even your HRD manager does that. There are times when it is more economical to buy one than to make it yourself. Of course, you have to take the time to get to know the program so you can decide if it is really what you want. Your HRD manager can be a help to you on this, but the final decision should be yours — particularly if it is coming out of your budget.

How Do We Know What We Are Getting for Our Money?

As a manager, you always want to know what kind of return you are getting for the budget payments you authorize. This should be no different for HRD, though it may be a bit more difficult to determine than it is when you order a piece of machinery or some supplies.

The answer to this question depends, of course, on the kind of center you have. If there is a budget-item center, it is not your money unless you are currently working as the HRD manager. If there is either a cost or a profit center, the funding is directly in your hands as a line manager. Therefore, you not only should be interested, you should feel accountable and demand to know what you get for your HRD money.

A more detailed answer will be given in Chapter Seven, when we look at evaluation. For now, however, we are looking at just the accountability for the funding that is made available to HRD (that is, what HRD does with its money rather than how it benefits you). You should determine at the outset *why* you want that information — and you should make that determination *before* you make any funding available. Your HRD manager should be alerted to what kind of financial information you want and when you want it.

Then you have to decide what you will do with that information. You probably get more information now than you know what to do with, so the temptation is to refrain from asking for more. This is not healthy for the HRD function, the organization, or your role as a manager. Any time you must make a decision about allocating financial resources, you should also be asking what is to be done with those resources. You may not be interested in the salaries of the HRD staff or their administrative expenses; what you want to know is what it has cost you for their services. Later on, you want to be able to compare that figure with the benefits that accrued to you (or your unit) by paying for those services.

Why Does HRD Cost So Much?

This question can also be asked another way: what will it cost me if I do *not* provide HRD? Your employees learn, but they may be learning the wrong things. By providing organized learning programs, as needed, you can reduce some costs, improve quality, and provide the work force you need.

HRD costs because it requires the services of competent people. Of course, as with any expenditure, you can seek the lowest cost, but that may prove more costly in the long run. That does not mean that you should not investigate comparative costs, but it does mean that you have to have some idea of what you are buying and what the results will be.

When purchasing a packaged program or contracting with an external supplier, some of the obvious costs are very explicit. You pay a set amount and get a specific program or service. The difficulty is that the cost does not stop there. You also should include the cost of travel, if it is required. There is also a cost in the lost work time of those in the learning program.

All of this can seem like a large cost, and it is. You should not be lulled into thinking that HRD is cheap. It is not. When thinking about the cost of HRD, what you have to consider is, what is the alternative?

What Facilities Does HRD Require?

In addition to funding, HRD requires facilities. Where HRD is being provided at the job site, by you or somebody delegated by you, there may not be a need for any special facility. For many HRD programs, however, some kind of special facility is required, if only to insulate the learners from job pressures.

The kind of facility needed depends on the types of HRD programs that will be offered. For some technical programs, it may be necessary to use equipment that requires a special facility. This may be due to safety requirements, health factors, or company security. It may also be required because of the nature of the equipment. When computers came into general use, some HRD managers tried to just plug them in at the learning facility, and this produced some electrical disasters. It soon became clear that special wiring or rewiring was required if computers were to be used in the HRD facility.

There are two kinds of space requirements that influence the facility situation: dedicated space and shared space. Both refer primarily to the space needed for the learning programs. The administrative space would be similar to any other administrative area in the organization.

What is dedicated space? Dedicated space is space used exclusively for HRD programs. This may mean classrooms, breakout rooms (small rooms for small-group work), practice areas, and even some recreational space for coffee breaks and just relaxation. There will be special provisions for instructional equipment (such as projectors) and storage space for materials. It is unlikely that this space would be used for any other purpose, although there are some possibilities, such as staff meetings of other units. The space, however, should be under the control of the HRD manager.

The location of dedicated space depends on many factors. In some organizations, it might just be a well-defined area either within the regular space occupied by the organization or in a separate building. In recent years, some large companies have built corporate centers, sometimes called either conference or education centers, that are devoted exclusively to HRD programs.

What is shared space? Shared space is a facility to be used by the HRD unit and other units of the organization as well. In this kind of situation, it is less likely that provision can be made for some of the special needs of HRD operations. It will be necessary to compromise since the facility has to be flexible enough to meet the needs of the various units of the company that expect to use it. The control and scheduling of the space will generally not be in the HRD manager's office. As with other units, the HRD manager will have to request the space as needed.

An alternative used by some organizations is to allow the HRD manager to rent space outside the organization. This works well when the HRD programs do not have a continuing need for space and when there is ample space within a reasonable distance from where the potential learners are situated.

When the HRD operation does need space on a continuing basis, it is often possible to arrange for a long-term contract for that space with a suitable hotel or motel. If only sporadic use will be made of the facility, a long-term contract may not be feasible, and the HRD manager will just have to compete with other organizations and groups for space. Some hotels and motels advertise themselves as conference centers but actually have merely function rooms that they convert into meeting rooms. Obtaining audiovisual equipment can become expensive and uncertain unless the facility has its own or knows of a reputable source.

Why Should I Be Concerned About HRD Equipment?

Obviously, the HRD manager is the one who should be the most concerned about HRD equipment. As a line manager, however, you also have some concerns. One of these springs from the limited funding that is generally available in any organization. You want to be sure that the HRD unit is getting the equipment it needs but is not overstocking. As noted earlier, this can be a tendency in a budget-item center whenever the HRD unit has extra money that it feels obliged to spend before the end of the year.

Should I Have Any HRD-Dedicated Equipment in My Unit?

If you are conducting any learning programs within your unit, you may want to have some equipment dedicated to that purpose. You should be sure, however, that there is no unnecessary duplication with what the central HRD has. On the other hand, it could be that both you and the central HRD unit are missing some important pieces of equipment that would enhance the learning situation.

What Kind of HRD Equipment Might I Want to See in My Organization?

The real question here is, what equipment is *needed* for HRD in this organization? If the HRD manager does not ask you this question, you should be asking it of him or her. You should also ask two other questions: is the equipment we are considering up-to-date, and is it what is necessary? You want your HRD unit to be able to deliver the best learning possible, as effectively as possible — that is, within the shortest period of time consistent with the objectives that you have agreed upon for that learning. It may be as simple as having the appropriate tables and chairs, or as sophisticated as the latest equipment for videodisk presentations.

Why Is It Important That the HRD
Equipment Be Up-to-Date and Relevant?

The second point here is the more important one — you want to be sure that the equipment being used in the HRD center is relevant to what is being used on the job in your department. An incident that illustrates this point occurred in the oil industry in a country where that industry was nationalized. The oil companies were very proud of their HRD centers, where education was provided for newly recruited employees being prepared to be posted to one of the operating companies. The HRD manager of one particular center was especially proud of his equipment, which had been received from one of the operating companies. The machines were in excellent working order; however they were *not* the machines the learners would be working with when they went on the job. The machines helped instruct the learners in the essentials of welding, but when those learners were assigned to the actual work sites, they needed training on equipment they had never seen before!

How about your organization? Is your HRD unit using equipment that is exaxctly like what is being used in your department, or are you going to be dissatisfied with the employees you get after they have been through the HRD program? Will you then have to provide additional on-the-job training to make up for the lack of relevant equipment in the HRD unit?

You should be involved in discussions related to the purchase of equipment even when it does not come out of your budget. If your HRD manager does not invite you into those discussions, it is within your position as a line manager to ask for that inclusion. Usually, it is not that the HRD manager wants to leave you out; rather, it is that you may not previously have indicated any interest in this essential decision-making process.

What Is a Corporate Conference Center?

As noted earlier, some large companies have special, dedicated HRD facilities that go by a variety of names, the most common of which are corporate conference center and corporate training center. The list of organizations with dedicated HRD centers includes IBM, Xerox, Motorola, Travelers Insurance, the U.S. Postal Service, and Eastman Kodak—to name just a few. The list is quite long and appears to be growing. For the most part, these centers are owned by large corporations, but we suspect that some smaller ones also have such centers, though they do not get quite the same degree of publicity.

What Is My Relationship to a Corporate Conference Center?

As a line manager, you have several different kinds of relationships to such a learning center. If your company is planning to build one, you might be asked to sit on the committee that works with the architects. If it already exists, you might be asked to serve on the advisory panel or some similar body that provides guidance and oversight to the facility. At a minimum, you will be attending sessions at the center or sending some of your subordinates to that center.

Does My Organization Need an HRD Conference Center?

There are many reasons for organizations to have their own facilities, and if your organization has one you should try to determine why it does. They are expensive, running into the millions of dollars just to construct. Operating them can also be costly, so why does your organization have one—or why is one being considered?

One reason may be that this allows the organization to set up exactly the kind of learning climate that is wanted. For example, for many years, liquor was not permitted at the IBM centers. Other corporate centers have their own regulations and practices that serve to communicate the culture of the organization.

Another reason is the economic one. If your organization has a very active HRD program, it may be more economical to have your own facility rather than to contract out for HRD services. Of course, this can have a reciprocal effect—once the facility is in operation, the HRD manager of that facility may

have to sell as many programs as possible to make the center
cost-effective. Some HRD corporate center managers have met
this need by renting out parts of the facility when they are not
being used. This has advantages and limitations, but generally
you need not be concerned about them unless you are a member of the center's advisory board or some similar oversight
group. Then, you want to be sure that it really is *your* organization's conference center and not just a center run by your organization to make a profit by renting space to external groups.

Does a Conference Center Have
Anything Other Than Meeting Rooms?

Many of the corporate conference centers provide sleeping rooms
as well as meeting rooms. This is particularly helpful when you
have a multi-site organization and are bringing people in from
different parts of the United States or from other countries. Not
only can it be cost-effective, it also allows the participants to
meet each other informally after the instructional day is over.
Of course, given this type of facility, it is always possible to have
evening sessions if so desired.

Who Keeps HRD's Financial Records?

No matter what type of HRD center is used, financial records
must be kept. This is no problem today, given the various computer software programs. The essential point is that the HRD
financial records should be kept in the same format as other corporate records. This is fairly common today, with most HRD
financial transactions being recorded in the organization's central record-keeping facility.

There may, however, be some factors unique to an organization's HRD financial records that necessitate combining
figures from the HRD budget with those of other activities in
order to get the best financial reading available.

Will I Have to Maintain Any HRD Financial Records?

As a line manager, you may be asked to maintain some kinds
of records that relate to the HRD financial picture. For exam-

ple, you may have to provide a dollar figure for time spent by your employees in learning situations (including the cost of travel and per diems). You want that data so that you can have some idea of what HRD is costing you even if the organization is using a budget-item center for HRD. You might also need such information if you are asked to serve on the corporate HRD advisory panel or similar activity related to HRD.

If you are conducting any extensive on-the-job training, you will want to have some financial records to reflect the use of resources in that situation. It may be that you have delegated one of your subordinates to devote a given number of hours each week to on-the-job training. If so, you would want to be able to charge that time to your HRD expense so that it did not distort your operational costs.

Who Keeps the Records on HRD's Physical Operations?

This will depend on whether or not there is a dedicated HRD facility. If there is no such facility, then the essential records may be maintained outside the HRD unit. Indeed, you as a line manager may not even be involved in looking at the record of the physical operations, such as use of space or equipment.

If there is a corporate HRD center, as discussed earlier, then the person in charge of that facility will be expected to keep records. Your concern may be to see how your unit's activities are reflected in those records.

Linking Employee Learning with Performance Improvement

Why Do I Need to Know How My Employees Learn?

Providing learning for your employees is one of the responsibilities of every manager of people. That does not mean that you have to know everything about the area of adult learning, but you need to know something about how adults learn and how that learning relates to work performance.

The need to know is fairly obvious when training is the objective but (as noted in Chapter Two) more difficult to identify when education is the objective, for it may not be clear who the future manager will be or when the employee will be expected to move to the future job. When it comes to development, you need only be minimally concerned since it is not job related. Therefore, the major focus of the discussion in this chapter will be on training.

Learning can be divided into that which takes place away from the job site and that which takes place at the job site, usually called on-the-job training.

If I Send Employees Away for Training, Why Do I Still Need to Be Concerned?

Being sent away from the job for training may mean being sent to another room in the same building, or to another building, or to another city, or to another country. The training program can be one conducted by your organization or one provided by an outside supplier. It is important that being sent away from the job for training is not viewed as being rejected or abandoned.

You, the manager, should be involved in the entire process: during the selection of the employee who is to go to training, during the training, and in some positive way when the employee returns. Therefore, it is important for you to know what kind of learning experience is being provided, how it relates to the objectives of the program (which you should have had a hand in determining), and what kind of different (hopefully improved) job performance you can expect when the employee returns. As the employee discusses the experience, you should know how it was organized, what kinds of learning strategies were used, and how it was evaluated.

On-the-Job Training Is Easy, So Why Should I Be Concerned?

For some managers, offering on-the-job training is easy, but not for all. It should involve much more than just showing somebody how to do a job, and it certainly goes beyond giving directions. Real on-the-job training is an organized learning experience even though it does not use a classroom or a professional instructor. It must be organized by you, although you can certainly call on your HRD people for help. Unfortunately, this is too seldom done.

Even when you use your HRD people as a resource, however, you should still know enough about how adults learn so you can ask the right questions and understand the answers. You need to know something about the various learning strategies available and what special equipment or materials will make your efforts easier and more productive.

How Does Learning Relate to Performance?

There is a continuing controversy about the relationship between learning and performance. You do not need to get involved in that controversy, but you should recognize that it exists so that you are not confused by the proponents of one position or another. There are those who contend that learning includes a change in behavior or performance, while there are others who are equally persistent in saying that people can learn and still not change their performance. We tend to side with those who hold the latter point of view.

Our position is based on many years of seeing people learn and then fail to apply that learning on the job. In these cases, there was no question that the learners had achieved a new level of knowledge, attitude, or skill. When they returned to the job, however, their performance was the same as they had exhibited before they went for training. In such a case, it is easy to criticize the training, but that is neither helpful nor fair.

How often have you heard a manager say to an employee just returned from training, "OK, you had your vacation. Now, get back to work and make up the lost time!" The message is, "I do not care what you learned; you will still do it my way, the way you did it before."

It should be understood that learning brings about the *possibility* of a change in performance. Whether that change takes place depends to a great degree on what you do to reinforce the learning on the job and whether you provide opportunities for the employee to actually use the new knowledge as near to the completion of the learning program as possible. The longer the delay in applying the new learning, the greater the possibility that the learning will be forgotten. Of course, that is one of the major problems with education. There can be a long time lag between the learning experiences and the moment when the employee is placed on the new job. In the interim, a good deal of learning can be forgotten.

What Is Andragogy?

There are many different approaches to learning, even when we are only concerned with the adult as the learner. One of the most common of these is termed *andragogy*, and one of its leading exponents has been Malcolm Knowles. (For more on this and other learning theories, see Knowles's book *The Adult Learner: A Neglected Species*. [3rd ed.] Houston, Texas: Gulf Publishing, 1984.) At one time, the thinking was that this was a way of distinguishing between learning for children (pedagogy) and learning for adults (andragogy). More recently, andragogy has been applied to a concept of learning that might be applicable to children but is very important for adults.

The main points to consider when providing learning for adults are the following: intent to apply, experience, and self-direction. The following discussions of these points synthesize the work of Knowles and other researchers in this field.

Do my employees really intend to apply the learning? The intention to apply learning highlights the difference between a child and an adult in our society. A child is generally exposed to learning with the understanding that *someday* he or she will need this learning. An adult is generally more concerned with immediacy — how can I use it *now*?

How soon learning will be used brings us back to the difference between training and education. Training is called for if your employee needs to be able to use what has been learned right away. Education is called for if the employee intends to use the learning sometime in the future. Education requires that the adult (your employee) have a future orientation. There are those who are more comfortable dealing with quick results (sometimes called immediate gratification), and they can be expected to have some difficulty with education.

In learning where development is the objective, the intent to apply the learning on the job is not relevant.

How does experience come into the learning picture? Generally, the older the employees are, the greater the experience they can bring to the learning situation. This can be an advantage because most learning takes place by association. That is, new learning is built on what the individual has learned or experienced in the past. Of course, the experienced employee should not be forced to repeat what has already been learned.

A problem arises when the employee has not had any experience related to the objective of the present learning. It then becomes necessary to create artificial situations or other kinds of vicarious learning as the basis for the new learning.

With any kind of learning one has to consider what the learner's previous experience may have been like. If a particular employee had a negative school experience, being assigned to another learning experience may be seen as just another possibility for failure. That does not mean you should not send the employee for training, but it does mean that the preparation for that experience will be different than it would be for an employee who had had several previous successful experiences in learning situations.

What is meant by self-direction? Generally, adults in our society want to have some influence over situations they are in. This is not news to you — you probably use this knowledge in making assignments so that your people can exert some influence and control over the work situation. The same should apply to the learning situation. The more your employees can influence or control the learning situation — that is, the more self-direction they are allowed — the greater the possibility of a profitable learning experience.

There are various ways to promote self-direction, such as involving your people in developing the learning experience and even allowing for some self-selection, when appropriate.

Can I expect all my employees to be self-directing? Some people just do not have the drive or desire to be self-directing. They prefer to have others tell them what to do. Perhaps they prefer that others make decisions for them so that they do not have to bear any responsibility for the results. To force them to be self-directing in a learning situation can produce results that are just opposite to the learning objectives.

It is also possible that a person's degree of self-direction may have to be considered in the light of differences in cultures. Given the increasing diversity of the work force in the United States, it is very possible that you have some employees for whom being self-directing is counter-cultural. It may be that they believe in destiny — that things are preordained. Therefore, to be self-directing is to be going against one's destiny. Alternatively, they may have learned from their culture that those in charge know it all (or they would not be in charge). Therefore, to be self-directing is a challenge to those in charge.

Difficulties in self-direction arising from either personality or culture can be dealt with positively. How to deal with them is one of those items to discuss with your HRD people, since the approach will vary from one organization to another.

What Are Instructional Strategies?

This is a term that has emerged to cover the great variety of activities and products that are useful in helping adults to learn, particularly in work situations. One reason for this umbrella term is that there has been a lack of agreement as to whether something is a method or a technique. As the difference does not seem to be important, some of us have sidestepped the definitional problem and instead devoted our efforts to identifying those strategies that can be useful.

For the manager, it is important to know some of them so as to be able to communicate with the HRD people. It can also be of help when a manager must make some choices among the instructional strategies to be used in on-the-job training. Therefore, in place of a long list with examples, the following discussion will focus on the major trends at this time. (A list of over eighty instructional strategies, with brief definitions, can be found in Leonard Nadler's book *Designing Training Programs.* Reading, Mass.: Addison-Wesley, 1982.)

What Are Some of the Major
Trends in Instructional Strategies?

As in so many areas of work, the major trend is technology. A good deal of what has emerged enables a manager to provide much more HRD on the job than ever before. At this time HRD people are still being overwhelmed by the technological advances that can affect learning situations.

The instructional strategies we will discuss here all have a significant value to the manager because they can be provided at the job site. This appears to be part of a larger trend to provide as much learning on the job as possible. This should not be seen as a criticism of learning away from the job, as there is certainly a place for that kind of learning. It emphasizes, however, that too often managers have utilized learning away from the job not because it was better, but because it allowed them to avoid being involved. But managers must be involved, and the newer instructional technologies make on-the-job learning much more available than in the past.

This certainly does not mean that all learning must or should take place on the job. For some learning objectives, it can be much more helpful to provide learning away from the job — for example, if it would help the employee to learn in a group composed of other employees from different parts of the same organization. If your organization uses project or task groups, learning with people from other parts of the organization can contribute to the effectiveness of those groups.

There are other reasons to use instructional strategies away from the job. Some apply to you, some do not. Therefore, it is suggested that you discuss this alternative with your HRD people, who should be able to explain when an instructional strategy is best conducted away from the job site.

The following questions and answers will relate to just a few selected strategies you should be familiar with, such as computers, video disks, and job aids.

How can I use the computer to provide instruction for my people? The computer, as an instructional strategy, has been with us since about the middle 1960s. Its impact, of course, has been growing since the end of the 1970s, when the personal computer was introduced. Since then, there have been many advances, and many more can be expected. (An overview of the uses of the computer for learning can be found in Angus Reynolds's article "Computers and HRD." In L. Nadler and Z. Nadler [eds.], *The Handbook of Human Resource Development.* [2nd ed.] New York: Wiley, 1990.)

The most important part of the computer, for learning purposes, is the software. That is the material that goes into the computer to make it produce something — in this case a learning program. Software packages come and go very rapidly. Some are in the form of games, such as those dealing with making business decisions. Others deal with various forms of knowledge and attitude. It is neither possible nor necessary to list relevant programs; they change too rapidly, usually for the better. Your instructional materials developer should be able to help you find what you need for a particular situation.

There are people working on making the computer as helpful in the skills as it already is in the knowledge area. Rather than just relying on the traditional software, we can couple the computer with other forms of technology (see the discussion below on video disks).

What computer software should I buy? First of all, not all software has to be bought by you. It could be purchased by your HRD unit, or it could be a pool purchase made with other managers, which helps keep the cost down.

You can access that software fairly easily. If your company has a large mainframe computer, it may contain a good deal of software that should be readily available to you. If, in your company, the emphasis is on the personal computer, you can still get access to software far beyond what you yourself might purchase. To do this, you would need a modem, which is a device that enables you to hook up by telephone to computers in other places, both within and outside of your organization.

What is a video disk? One of the significant recent technological advances has been in joining the computer to video in what is called the video disk. This became available in the early 1970s but just did not gain acceptance. By the beginning of the 1990s, however, it had revived and now seems to be gaining acceptance. It provides a significant opportunity to utilize resources that have not previously been available, particularly at the job site. It brings together combinations of the computer, videotape, still photographs, sound, and other resources.

To make the most effective use of this instructional strategy, you may need to work not only with your HRD people but also with others in the organization. This can make video disks much more cost-effective, and cost is a major concern with video-disk technology.

The video disk has proven very valuable in providing sales training programs, as well as other programs that rely on product knowledge. It can also be used to help build skills in working with other people. It has many advantages when it is important to the learner to actually see and vicariously experience another environment or to experience what cannot be provided in-house.

What is a job aid? You have probably been using job aids informally in many of your management practices. Job aids are different devices and materials that enable you to provide quick and brief instruction about an element of a job. A job aid essentially shows when, where, and how to do the particular task or job. There are times when a job aid will suffice and a full training program is not required.

Job aids include such items as charts, audiotapes, forms, models, and checklists. They can range from a single picture or page to a whole book, from an index card to a large colored poster. There are some who contend that these are not instructional strategies but just items providing information. At this point, it does not seem helpful for us to contribute to that discussion. Rather, recognize that job aids can be a very valuable way for you to help your people learn simple and repetitive tasks.

You can make your own job aids, but that can be time-consuming and costly. In a large organization, you can use your HRD unit to find out what is available in other parts of your organization that could be helpful to you. As needed, your HRD staff might also be able to help you create suitable job aids.

What are some other instructional strategies? The list can go on and on — there are well over a hundred of them. With advances in technology they keep changing, as you would expect. It is not necessary for you to try to keep up-to-date. Rather, your HRD staff should be able to update you as necessary.

If you are interested, you can ask your HRD people to explain strategies such as team building, transactional analysis, neurolinguistic programming, and right-brain/left-brain approaches. Help them understand that your goal is not to be an expert on these and other strategies but to know something of what they are about.

Is the Assessment Center Something I Can Use?

The assessment center is an interesting approach that can be used either for selection of personnel or for identification of learning needs. Unfortunately, sometimes you will find people using that approach without making the necessary distinction.

The assessment center utilizes people who are trained assessors, and you yourself may have served in such a role. The employees being assessed are usually those being considered for promotion or transfer to a new job. The center presents problems and situations much like those actually found on the job, and the employee is asked to respond and take appropriate action. The assessors then rate the performance of the employee. The performance of the employee usually will be low risk, an attempt to provide what the assessors are looking for.

When used for HRD, the assessment center is somewhat the same in operation but much different in purpose. The objective is to identify learning needs, particularly skills that will be needed on a new job. The employee should be urged to take chances, as his or her potential is not being examined. Rather, the choice has already been made, and now the assessment center is being used to identify specific learning needs for the employee.

Evaluating the Effectiveness of HRD Programs and Activities

Is There a Difference Between Evaluation and Research?

There certainly is, and it is important to clarify that difference right at the beginning. The difference between the two can be stated very simply: evaluation tries to determine *what* happened, while research is concerned with *why* it happened. Every manager must be interested in finding out *what* happened as the result of an HRD experience, and therefore every manager must be involved in evaluation. When it comes to the *why,* a manager may be interested but probably lacks the resources (time, funds) to become involved. This chapter will focus only on evaluation.

Should I Leave Evaluation to the Experts?

You are already involved in evaluation, probably in many ways. For your staff, you probably do a performance evaluation. For quality control, you do a product evaluation. One form of evaluation is a budget review. You probably also do some evaluation when looking at how you have used facilities and funding for which you are responsible. From your own work you could probably list many more areas where you make evaluations, although you may not actually call your efforts "evaluations."

Since you probably have less experience in evaluating learning, you might want to consider using an expert to assist you there. However, you should not allow the expert to make decisions about how to use the evaluation results. You should be aware also that the evaluation of training cannot take place unless you are directly involved.

92

How Can the Experts Help Me?

There are many different ways to evaluate learning, and the experts can help you consider the various options. Recall that in Chapter Four there was a discussion of the HRD consultant as an expert. You might want to use just such an expert to help you understand the different types of evaluation that can be conducted and what you can expect of each. Then you should make the final decision as to which specific kind of evaluation you want conducted.

What Should I Want to Have Evaluated in HRD?

The two things that you should want evaluated are learning and performance. Obviously, these are related, but each needs to be considered separately.

If your HRD people are not clear *before* the program starts about what you will want to find out from evaluating each area, it may be impossible for you to get this information when the program ends. Because evaluation deals with change, your HRD people will need your help to determine the prospective learner's current level of performance. That way they can provide you with evaluation information about what has changed and let you know what changes you can expect when the employee returns to the job. (Later in this chapter, training, education, and development will be considered separately in relation to evaluation.)

What Do I Need to Know About
Evaluating Learning in an HRD Program?

An HRD learning program should have specific objectives. Frequently, these are stated as learning objectives, but as a manager you are more concerned with anticipated changes in performance than with whether the learning objectives have been met. If possible, your HRD people should state the objectives in terms of changed performance.

You should not, however, ignore the learning, since without that the performance cannot be expected to change. Therefore, you do want to know what your people learned. This information should be stated simply and clearly so that you will not have to wade through jargon. You want specific answers to the question, How do you know they have learned? There are various ways for your HRD people to tell you this, but you have to provide them with specific indications of the kind of data or information you want.

If the program objectives were not achieved, what are some of the next steps to be taken? This information should be part of the evaluation material you get, but it is your option to decide what you want to do about those who have not reached the learning objectives. Among your alternatives are retraining, reassigning, or firing the employee — or simply ignoring the problem and the employee.

In addition to learning the subject matter, your people may also have learned how to learn. If the evaluation can provide you with this kind of information, it can affect how you conduct on-the-job training in the future.

What Do I Need to Know About Performance Evaluation After the HRD Program?

This question deals with transferring the new knowledge from the learning situation to the work situation. You will want to know, through a systematic evaluation, whether the employee's performance has changed. You may also need to have some quantification — how much did performance change?

Too often a manager feels that once the employee has returned from the HRD program, the HRD unit should be out of the picture. Actually, this becomes counterproductive. If the HRD unit cannot determine whether performance actually changed, it has no way of knowing whether its efforts have been successful.

The evaluation of performance change must involve both the manager and the HRD people. Of course, the learner must also be involved, but it is the manager and HRD people who are accountable and who need to know enough about the change in performance to determine the relative success of the program.

How Do I Know If the Cost of the
HRD Program Was Worth the Result?

This is another way of asking about the cost-benefit ratio for HRD. To answer this question you must first know what poor performance costs you, and for some jobs this is easy. You can count the rejected material, or the need for additional service calls, and so on.

Cost becomes more difficult to determine when you are dealing with services. A salesperson who does not make a sale incurs a cost without any corresponding income. On the other hand, the loss may be due to factors that have nothing to do with performance, such as competitor pricing or market conditions. If the loss of that sale can be attributed to lack of product knowledge or sales techniques, then it may be possible to calculate some kind of cost.

In the end, you will have to decide whether providing learning will cost more than the benefits you can derive from it. If you did not make that decision before providing the learning, it should be done afterwards and used as the basis for future decision making.

I Have Heard of Hard Data and
Soft Data. What Is the Difference?

The words *hard* and *soft* refer to two different kinds of data or information that can be collected when evaluating an HRD program. The essential difference is that *hard* refers to quantitative data, things that can be counted or measured. *Soft* refers to qualitative data, where counting is not possible but observation can be effective. That is, after a training program, an individual can be observed to determine if his or her performance is up to standard.

For example, in a safety training program, the evaluation might be obtained by looking for hard data, such as a reduction in the number of accidents. This approach assumes, however, that all safety problems are amenable to training. If there are other factors contributing to safety problems that the training did not address, you might not see a change in the numbers. In this case, you might want to use the qualitative approach by observing whether the employees follow the safety procedures that were taught in the HRD program.

Which Kind of Data Is Better?

It is not possible to answer this question until you decide what you want to know. This in turn relates directly to the reason for the HRD program and the results you expect to see. When the objective of the HRD program is to increase the quantity of performance, and when the performance of the employee can be quantified, you would look for hard data — that is, numbers.

Is All Performance Quantifiable?

No, it is not. For example, look at the performance of most managers. It is generally not possible to quantify all executive, managerial, or supervisory performance. There have been continuing efforts to do this, but for the most part they have not been successful. However, if such behavior is quantified in your organization, then you can use the guidelines for that process to quantify changes in performance as a result of training.

In What Form Can I Expect the
Hard Data to Be Reported to Me?

As hard data deal with numbers, you can expect numbers. The numbers you get have been treated by various statistical procedures to make them more meaningful to you. There are times when HRD managers go overboard on this by using more statistics than are necessary. They might also use statistical measurements that are not familiar to you.

Of course, there are those HRD managers who will do that to show how much they know or how proficient they are in using statistics. Others are just so used to statistics that they do not stop to question whether you will understand them.

If you do not understand the statistics, do not hesitate to ask! After all, those statistics are part of the tools of HRD, and the HRD manager should be proficient in their use. Similarly, you use tools in your management functions of which the HRD manager may be woefully ignorant.

How About Reporting the Soft Data?

The soft data will generally, but not always, be more understandable. They usually take the form of narrative reports, journals, or other verbal assessments. Just as with statistics, it is possible for the HRD manager to give you more information than you need or give it in a form that is not understandable or usable. If you have any question about the reports you get, whether written or oral, do not hesitate to ask your HRD manager for clarification. The HRD staff are not trying to confuse you, but generally they have written so many reports that they may tend to use professional jargon.

Some line managers would rather get a one-page executive summary than a report. If that is what you want, then tell your HRD people so, and they should be able to provide it. Other line managers may not want the information predigested and look for the whole report. Your HRD people need to know what you will look for in a qualitative report before they even start gathering the data.

How Can I Find Out How HRD Improved Performance?

You have to start with the performance before HRD was provided. This is called *base-line data*. If you do not have any such data, it is not possible to show how performance has improved. If you do have that information, it is possible to compare performance after the HRD experience with the base-line data.

How Much Change Can I Expect HRD to Make?

HRD provides learning, and there are limits to how people can change as a result of learning. For example, if the job requires three hands, no amount of HRD will be able to bring about that change. Your expectations have to be realistic.

Who Sets the Objectives for an HRD Activity?

This should be a joint process involving at least you and the HRD people. You know what you want or need, and the HRD people should be working with you when they write the objectives for any HRD program.

When possible, the employee who is to go through the HRD program should also be involved, but sometimes this can prove quite costly. As with any other cost, you have to assess the relative value of involving the employees in setting the objectives that will produce changed performance.

The HRD people have many ways of writing objectives, but they need your help to set them. After the objectives are written, they should be given to you to review, to be sure that you still agree with them.

What Is a Good Learning Objective?

What do you want your employees to know or do after the program that they did not know or do before the program? The answer to this question will give you your learning objectives. Your HRD people can work on the precise wording of the learning objectives, but only after you have told them what you expect.

How Do HRD People Evaluate Learning?

There are many ways to do this, but almost all of them will include at least three elements: data gathering, analysis, and feedback.

The HRD people can gather the data—that is, get test results during and after the learning program. If you are concerned with performance, they can only get that data with your help, when your employees return to the job after the learning experience or move on to the new job.

Do not blame your HRD people if they provide you with an analysis that you cannot understand, particularly if you have not taken the time to discuss the evaluation with them before the learning program began. You should explore with them the different kinds of information and data you want, and then they can plan the data gathering and analysis accordingly — to meet your needs.

When Does Evaluation Take Place?

Evaluation can take place at many points during and after a learning program. Two words you may hear are *formative,* meaning that the evaluation takes place while the program is being conducted, and *summative,* meaning that the evaluation is done after the program is completed. (There are those, however, who use *formative* to mean that the evaluation takes place while the learning program is being designed. Check with your HRD people to determine how they are using the term.)

During the program, it is possible to evaluate only whether *learning* is taking place. Generally, you need not be concerned with this type of evaluation. It can, however, be used by instructors to help those learners who are having difficulty meeting the objectives.

The final evaluation should be in two phases. The first occurs at the end of the learning program and is designed to find out what the employees have learned and perhaps whether they can use the new learning to improve their performance — but still in the learning environment. The second phase is much more important, of course, and is designed to evaluate the new performance in the actual job situation.

Are There Differences in Evaluating Training, Education, and Development?

Yes, there are differences, and it is essential that you take them into account when considering evaluation. If this is not done, it may be impossible for you to get any useful evaluation data. The evaluation of each kind of learning is related to the time frame in which the learning will be implemented. Training focuses on learning for a present job, education for a future job. With development, there is no expectation of change in performance. Consequently, each must be evaluated differently. When this is not done, it is probable that the evaluation will not be very helpful to you.

How Does Evaluation Relate to Training?

This depends on why you sent the employee (or employees) for training. There can be many reasons for doing so, and the evaluation should relate directly to your reason for using training. If it was to correct a performance deficiency, you will want to evaluate the degree to which that deficiency has been corrected. If it was to have the employee perform differently because of new equipment or a new process, then the evaluation can take place only when the employee is assigned to the new equipment or when the new process is actually functioning in your unit.

Whatever the reason, you want to evaluate the employee's ability to exhibit the new performance on the job immediately. Of course, that means that you must provide a reasonable opportunity for the employee to demonstrate the new performance as soon after the end of the training program as possible.

Can I ask the HRD people to evaluate my employees for me during a training course? This is a delicate question and one that raises questions of ethics. During training, it can be expected that the learner will make mistakes, because that is one way that learning takes place. If the learner is concerned about being evaluated during training, however, the result could be hesitancy on the part of the learner to try out new performance. That would tend to make the training experience much less effective.

It is also possible that during training the learner might need to speak frankly about the job and the organization. If there is a possibility of being evaluated during the training program, with the results going back to you, it might hinder some of the learning experiences that have been planned.

However, there may sometimes be a good reason for wanting such an evaluation during training. When that is the case, it should be discussed with the HRD people and your employees before the training program is conducted or the employees are assigned to the program. If your employees are to be evaluated during the training program, they should know it beforehand.

Is there any situation when it is appropriate for me to get the evaluation results during the training program? There are some unique situations in which this would be appropriate. If the new behavior is greatly concerned with safety, it may be important for you to know during the training program whether a particular employee is able to comply with the safety requirements.

When the training is related to a new piece of equipment, it may become obvious during the training program that a particular employee will not be able to achieve the skill level necessary. This commonly happens when there is new technology involved. It would be best for all concerned for the employee to recognize that the appropriate skill level will not be achieved. At that time, you should explore possible alternatives with the employee.

What should I do with the evaluation results of training? It is not enough just to get the results — you should also use them. If the evaluation shows that the program has been successful, why not share that information with the HRD unit? It might also be helpful to share your understanding of the evaluation with your employees — they should know whether you are satisfied with the new performance that resulted from the training program.

If you are not satisfied with the results, let your HRD people know that too. If you do not, how can they possibly improve and be more helpful to you next time?

How Does Evaluation Relate to Education?

Where education is concerned, you may be involved in evaluation at different times. You may be involved before the learning begins, when you send one of your people to be educated for a new job in your unit. You may be involved afterwards in finding out whether the employee has learned the appropriate new performance. Obviously, you cannot determine this until the employee is actually placed in the new job.

You must consider the time lapse between the end of the education experience and the beginning of any opportunity for the employee to exhibit the new performance. It is possible for the employee to forget the new learning, at least in part, if there is no opportunity to use it between the end of the education program and placement in the new job. Evaluating at the end of learning might be helpful, but it would not be a good indication of the long-term results of the education program.

When the objective is education, it is possible that the employee will leave your unit. In that case, you will not be involved in the evaluation on the new job.

On the other hand, you might receive an employee who was educated in order to be transferred to your unit. You might want to know something of the evaluation that took place at the end of education, but you should be more concerned with some form of immediate performance appraisal. This might indicate the need for refresher training for the employee.

How Does Evaluation Relate to Development?

As development is not job related, you will generally not be too interested in the evaluation of development-related learning.

One aspect of development evaluation, however, might be of interest to you. That is, has the employee shown an ability to learn? If so, it may mean that providing training will be relatively easy. If the employee has shown any learning difficulties, you may have to plan to have your HRD people provide some special learning skills before making training available to that employee.

Being a Supportive Partner in HRD Efforts

Why Should I Be Interested in Providing Organizational Support for HRD Activities?

You should at least be interested, but you must go beyond interest and provide support. Without organizational support, HRD cannot possibly exist as either a specific unit or a defined activity. HRD is important to the life of every organization, and managers need access to HRD. If you do not support it inside your organization, you must then be prepared to pay for it from outside your organization.

If you have any doubts about its value, just ask yourself what your organization would be like if it did not provide learning for employees at all levels — including you. You would have trouble getting your work done, it would be impossible for your people to work at the level necessary for an efficient organization, and you would not be preparing efficiently for the changes that always occur.

Should the Same Support Be Provided for All HRD Activities?

Once again the distinction between training, education, and development becomes essential. Most of the discussion that follows will focus on training, for that is the largest area of HRD activity and one where your support is essential. However, education and development also need to be considered, as does HRD consulting.

Do I Need to Be Committed to Supporting HRD?

Yes, you must be committed to HRD; moreover, it is important that your commitment be clear to everybody in the organization. However, commitment alone is not enough — you must also be involved.

What Is the Difference Between
Commitment and Involvement?

There is a great deal of difference between the two. Commitment is a *promise,* while involvement is *action.* When you support training, it is fine to start with the promise, but then you must follow up with specific actions showing your involvement. The actions you take are crucial in showing everybody that you support HRD. The specific actions required from you will differ depending upon the type of HRD program and the practices in your organization. You may have to initiate some new practices showing involvement if this has not been the pattern in your organization in the past.

How Should I Support Training?

Your support depends, in part, on the models your HRD people are using to set up their HRD operation, and particularly on how they design training programs. One model stresses organizational involvement and prescribes specific actions in pretraining, during training, in job linkage, and in follow-up. Let us look at how your actions in each of these areas can support training. (Of course, not all of these areas will apply to your organization.)

What should I be doing in regard to organizational involvement? This depends on your level in the organization. If you are a high-level manager, you probably at least make some general statements about training to show your commitment, but you also should be taking positive actions, such as providing the needed resources. While it is of prime importance to help develop and support policy statements regarding training, you should also help develop and implement the regulations that can move the organization to involvement.

You must expect to give some of your own time to those efforts. Of course your time is valuable, and you probably need time for many of your other activities. But the people in your organization will be looking at how much time you give to supporting HRD. If all you do is write memos stating support, it may not be sufficient.

An essential aspect of support is funding. You can show your support for HRD by ensuring that there is a budget and that funds are available as needed. This does not mean issuing a blank check, but the HRD people should not have to go begging for funds. You should also be involved in determining how the HRD unit will be made accountable for those funds.

You should participate in such activities as a company-wide HRD committee or review groups related to HRD programs. As needed, you should be prepared to delegate some of these activities to other people on your staff, but not to the degree that you no longer attend meetings.

What should I do as part of pre-training? Before the training begins, there are many things you can do. The first is to review the training course outline and the material to be taught to be sure they are pertinent to the needs of your employees. Most important are the actions you can take regarding the learners — your employees. They should be selected very carefully. This will take your time, but it can ensure that the right people are being sent for training.

The learners should be given as much advance notice as possible. Although training can be considered just another job assignment, it requires that the individual perform differently as a learner than as an employee on the job. You should also prepare the work situation in a variety of ways. Probably the most important is to arrange for coverage while the employee is away from the job site.

In Chapter Seven there is a discussion of evaluation and how you relate to that activity. Planning for evaluation should start now, as part of the pre-training support that you can give.

You must tell the HRD people what you want evaluated and perhaps even work with them on some aspects of the evaluation design process.

What should I do during the training? Even while your employee is in a training program, there are various ways you can show your support. An essential one is to avoid interruptions. Unless there is a severe crisis, you should not pull your employee out of the program. Even sending messages to be picked up at coffee breaks can prove disruptive and signal a lessening of your support.

Training programs come in a variety of patterns. In some, your employees may be away from the job for many days. If that is the case, plan to maintain contact as one way of showing your support. You can arrange to meet with the employee or delegate this to one of your senior staff. If the employee is attending a training program in another city, a long-distance phone call or fax can be a way of showing your support.

At times, the HRD staff may invite you to take part in a training program by giving a talk, sharing some information, or in some other way being a resource person. Your actual presence, rather than an excuse or a substitute, is another way of showing your support.

Some training programs have a formal closing with an awarding of certificates, a lunch, or some other kind of ceremony. This is more common in countries other than the United States, but as the U.S. workplace becomes more internationalized, such closings can be expected more frequently. When one or more of your employees is completing a training program, you might be invited to attend, and your presence is another indication of your involvement in supporting training. If you have not been invited, your query to your HRD people can show that you are interested and actively seeking involvement.

What is job linkage? Job linkage is the activity, during training, of preparing the learner to return to the job. This is helpful in all training programs and crucial when the training is conducted away from the job site and for an extended period of time. The training site may be in a different building or in a different city. The important point is that during training the learner does not return to the job site and therefore is not up-to-date on changes, including the ordinary ones that take place day to day. This can inhibit performance change when the learner does return to the job.

Your involvement here can serve other purposes as well. It will enable you to get a good handle on what your employees are learning and how that learning can and should be used back on the job. It sets the psychological goals as well as the objectives for what happens when your employee returns to the job.

How can I assist in job linkage? There are several things you can do, and they should all take place during the training. You should work with your HRD people to design and plan the relevant experiences so that they are congruent with the training rather than being in conflict or irrelevant.

One important job-linkage activity that should take place near the end of the training experience is to review the goals of the training with your employee and to clarify just what you expect when that employee returns. This includes planning for evaluation back on the job and letting your employee know how that evaluation will be conducted. This helps the employee prepare to use the learning after returning to the job.

Ritual plays an important part in many of the things we do and can be very helpful in job linkage. The returning employee should not just show up or slink back from the training with guilt at having been away while the others were working. A ritual (event) should be planned that celebrates the employee's return. It need not be a big affair, and it should not be out of proportion to the situation. Your challenge is to devise something that is appropriate and observable.

One possibility is to arrange for the newly trained employee to share the results of the training with others. This could be done through demonstration or discussion, whichever is more appropriate. This has the added advantage that you may get a multiplier effect — you sent only one employee to training, but others can also benefit from the learning experience.

What should I be doing as follow-up? Follow-up has several dimensions, but it should not be confused with evaluation. During follow-up you should make sure that the returned employee has ample opportunity to utilize the new performance. This provides you with the opportunity for additional and positive communication with your employees, particularly those recently returned from training.

One of the interesting results of learning — one you may have experienced yourself — is that the more you learn, the more you realize what else you need to learn. At some time after the training, perhaps in several weeks, you should meet with the returned employee to see what other learning needs may have surfaced.

What Support Should I Give to Education for My Present Employees?

It is much more difficult to show involvement with education than it is with training. To start with, you have to believe in the need for education to prepare your people for promotions or transfers. This means you have to agree to lose your good people as they move on to other jobs in your organization. You can do this for selfish reasons — if people in the organization do not have the opportunity to change jobs, they may choose to leave the organization, and the pool of good people who could move into your unit could be severely reduced.

You should work with your HRD and other human resource people in choosing those employees who can benefit the most from education. You should help prepare them for the education experience and avoid making them feel guilty because they will be leaving you.

There are times when an employee goes for HRD education and then returns to your unit. In that case, you sent the employee for a learning experience to provide for upgrading or promotion within the unit. In such a situation, your support would be very much like that for training.

When an employee has been in an HRD education program where the ultimate objective is a transfer or promotion out of the unit, the type of support will be much different. In that situation, it is important to provide for the employee to return to the job currently held while waiting for the transfer or promotion. During that interim time, it is important that you do not make the employee feel like a lame duck. The employee should be treated the same as prior to the education experience, though you will obviously be making provision for a replacement.

If the employee is going on to another supervisor, you might want to meet with that supervisor and your employee in order to facilitate the move. After all, you would appreciate such assistance if you were the new supervisor or the educated employee.

What Support Should I Give to Education for Employees Who Will Be Coming to Me?

In some situations you will know there are employees being educated who will be moving into your unit. Why wait until they get there? While they are still in the education program, you should be making contact with them. This should be done with the full knowledge of the present supervisor. Not only will such action facilitate the movement, but it will also show your support of education as a way of helping employees realize the value of internal mobility.

What Support Should I Give to Development?

It is doubtful if you need to give any support to development programs. Do not, however, sabotage them. If your company has a policy to provide development, you are expected to support that policy.

If your company does not have any policy on development — and most do not — then you have to decide how much and what kinds of support you want to give to that activity. For example, you can release employees according to agreed-upon ground rules to take part in development experiences. Usually, you will not be expected to use your funds to provide development — but it is something you might want to consider.

What Support Should I Give to HRD Consulting?

In addition to the more obvious organized learning experiences (training, education, development), HRD also provides another kind of learning experience: consulting (see Chapter Four). Your support for this HRD activity is equally important.

One way to provide support is to avoid looking outside your organization each time you are seeking HRD consultant help. The external consultants may appear more glamorous, and they may even wine and dine you. After all, they need to market continually in order to get a consulting assignment from you. If your internal HRD consulting people did that, you would probably be very suspicious!

When your internal HRD consultants have been helpful to you, tell them so. Of course, if they have not been helpful you should let them know that too — directly. They should not have to figure this out by seeing you choose external consultants over them.

Are There Any Other Ways That I Can Support HRD?

There are indeed other ways, and you will find them articulated in other parts of the book under different headings. There, the support you can provide will be spelled out more specifically.

Placing HRD Strategically in the Organization

The underlying assumption in this chapter is that HRD is provided in your organization through internal means. Specifically, in your organization there exists a unit (or units) whose purpose it is to serve your HRD needs. If you do not have any identifiable internal HRD unit or group, this chapter can still help you consider some of the alternatives.

Why Should I Be Interested in Where HRD Is Placed in My Organization?

The placement of HRD has an important impact on the availability of HRD services, on how you can use those services, and on how the HRD unit can serve your HRD needs. You might even, at some point, be asked your opinion about where the HRD unit should be located. The decision on placement may be in the hands of others, but if you are not at least somewhat involved, you may find that a decision has been made that is not helpful to you. The placement of that unit has many implications for how HRD can serve you and what you can expect from it.

Should There Be One HRD Unit or Many?

The answer to this depends on a variety of factors. One of them is the size of the organization. Large organizations, particularly multi-site organizations, tend to have many HRD units placed at strategic levels within the organization, such as at corporate headquarters and in various departments and plants. Small organizations tend to have only one unit to serve the entire organization, and they frequently rely on external resources to actually deliver HRD programs and activities.

We Have Never Had an HRD
Unit — What Can I Expect?

It is difficult to indicate the consequences of the placement decision, as there are many variables. An important one is how the decision arose to have an HRD unit. It is important for you to find out as much as you can about how that decision was made if you want to know what you can expect.

Where there has never been an HRD unit, its placement will probably reflect the problem that has generated the need for an HRD unit. If, for example, the need was evidenced in sales, then the HRD unit will probably be located in the sales department.

Why Might I Need an HRD Unit Now,
When There Was Not One Previously?

Previously, you may not have needed an HRD unit in your organization for a variety of reasons. The most common reason may be that HRD was readily purchased externally. For some manufacturing firms, a good deal of their HRD needs may have been met by suppliers of equipment who were required to provide the requisite training, and sometimes education as well. For other firms, HRD needs may have been met by informal on-the-job training. Many kinds of changes can make these arrangements no longer workable.

What If an HRD Unit Is Introduced Merely
Because One of Our Executives Made That Decision?

This happens all too often. The decision to create an HRD unit may arise when an executive goes to some kind of training program and discovers what HRD can contribute to your organization. In that case, the new unit will probably be located close to that executive. If you are fortunate enough to have executives who believe in participative management, they might ask your opinion as to placement. Then you will have to consider some of the factors that are discussed in the other questions about placement.

What Other Factors Can I Expect to Influence the Placement of HRD in My Organization?

Among the most important factors will be the types of programs needed, the individuals who are in key positions in your organization, and the value the organization places on people. There are many other factors, but they can be considered less important or more transient. For example, the state of the economy at a particular time or the financial position of your organization will influence the size and scope of HRD — and therefore the placement decision.

How Will the Various HRD Programs Affect Placement?

If there are many programs that are generic (offered generally throughout your entire organization), there will probably be a unit to provide those programs. That unit can be expected to be at the same place in the organization as other units that provide organization-wide services. However, some departments may have special needs not shared by others. It can be expected, then, that the HRD units providing such programs might be located within the departments they serve.

How Will Organizational Values and Culture Affect Placement?

If your organization places a high value on helping employees learn and grow, the HRD unit will probably be placed in a very visible part of the organization. Conversely, if your organization believes in hiring extensively from the outside and is not particularly concerned about turnover, then you can expect the HRD unit to be buried in the organization.

What If My Organization Is Not Interested in HRD?

Then there is no problem about placement, but there is a problem about how you get HRD services when you need them.

You will probably have to allocate funds in your budget to purchase HRD externally, as the need arises. It may also be necessary for you to assign somebody in your unit to keep track of those external HRD programs — the funds used, the people participating, and so on.

If There Is an HRD Unit in My Organization, Where Should It Be?

The assumption in this question is that you have a choice — that you will be asked. If so, there are several items to be considered: centralization, level, and overlap.

What is the difference between a centralized and a decentralized HRD unit? Being centralized or decentralized is not peculiar to HRD. This question also arises with other functions that have organization-wide implications, such as sales, shipping, purchasing, and payroll. For HRD, the question is whether all HRD functions should be provided through one unit (centralized) or a variety of units in different parts of the organization (decentralized).

Which is better — centralized or decentralized? There is no good answer to this question. Rather, you have to ask yourself, which will serve my HRD needs better? Note that this means you have to look at your HRD needs and have some idea of what they are.

If HRD is centralized, at what level should it be placed? This question is relevant if your organization is one that has the standard pyramidal hierarchy. Usually, in such organizations, the general or staff functions have been grouped (centralized) and placed near the top. For example, the various human resource functions (still sometimes called personnel) can be grouped into one unit.

There is a movement toward other organizational structures, one of which is called flat. That is, the pyramid may still exist, but it will be collapsed into many fewer levels. This tends to decentralize units. When centralization is still the rule in a flat organization, the level at which an HRD unit is placed becomes much less important.

When should HRD be decentralized? Decentralization can be a good idea if it reflects the general trend in your organization. An increasing number of organizations are setting up autonomous work groups or similar small internal units. Where this is the case, at least some of the HRD operation will be decentralized into those groups.

If the organization has several sites, particularly if they are distant from each other, it may be more economical to have decentralized HRD units rather than to try to provide all services from the corporate center.

Many multinational companies have moved toward decentralization. In addition to distance, the reasons for this trend include the desire to have HRD staff drawn from the host country and the need to ensure that the HRD materials do not conflict with the host country's culture.

To Whom Should the HRD Unit Report?

When the HRD unit reports to a vice president for human resources or some similar position, the emphasis will be on accounting for funds and reporting on projects related to human resources in general. When the HRD unit is reporting to a function officer, such as a sales manager, the reporting will probably focus on the effect of HRD programs on sales and salespeople.

Should I Try to Have an HRD Unit in My Part of the Organization?

Increasingly, managers are finding it helpful to have some kind of HRD capability in their individual work situations. Rather than an actual unit, there may simply be several individuals who have the ability to conduct required HRD programs. You should not expect those people, unless they are HRD professionals, to be able to actually design and evaluate programs.

Their contribution will probably be in being able to conduct programs that have been designed by others. Where you have continuing learning (probably training) needs in your part of the organization, you might consider an HRD unit composed of one or more of your people.

What Problems Might I Encounter
If I Have My Own HRD Unit?

For your own HRD unit to work effectively, the people doing the work must not only have basic competencies (as discussed in other chapters of this book) but must also keep up-to-date. This means that you have to make some of your budget available for activities that may not relate directly to your unit's objectives. In other words, you must be sure not to just assign people to do HRD and then not provide the needed resources.

A problem that frequently arises is upward mobility. Will your HRD people be able to move up in your part of the organization, or will upward mobility require transfer to another unit? Unfortunately, this consideration can encourage some managers to assign less-effective employees to the HRD unit — because it will not make much difference if they leave! This will diminish their ability to perform, and your whole HRD service will suffer.

Professional and Ethical Concerns in HRD

There are many issues pertaining to HRD that are of interest and concern to all managers, and in this chapter some of them will be addressed. It can also be anticipated that new issues will arise, since HRD is concerned with people in all aspects of their work life. In addition, there are many social and economic aspects of life that can be expected to have an impact on HRD.

What Is Happening to the Definition of HRD?

You are probably hearing the term HRD used in a wide variety of ways, by many people. It has become popular, but unfortunately not all those who use the term mean the same thing by it. One current tendency is to relabel a variety of human resource areas as "HRD"—the practice sometimes called "putting old wine in new bottles." The content does not change—only the label does.

Another tendency is to try to lump a number of different human resource activities together and label them "HRD." Some of those activities may actually be HRD, as the term is defined and used in this book. Others may be different areas of human resources grouped together with HRD. This is not helpful, but it allows the individual or organization to build a larger area of activity or attempt to embrace a larger group of clients. However, it frequently causes conflict with other existing human resource operations and functions. This tendency contributes to guerrilla warfare in the field generally—and can do the same in your organization.

Therefore, whenever you are approached by somebody to talk about HRD, you had best first ask that person to define what is meant by the term. By doing this right up front, you will avoid becoming embroiled in the confusion.

HRD Is Concerned with Behavioral Change, but Do We Have the Right to Change People's Behavior?

This important ethical question gained prominence toward the end of the 1980s in response to various HRD programs (called "new age" by some) that aroused serious controversy and criticism. The critics insisted that these HRD programs invaded individual rights by trying to change religious and personal values.

HRD cannot, and should not, avoid expressing values. The values of the employer should be explicitly reflected in your HRD programs. Indeed, it can be helpful for an employee to understand the values of the organization so that he or she can make an informed decision to stay or leave.

All learning brings about the possibility of behavioral change. As long as people are learning — learning anything — they can expect to change. What HRD has to avoid is forcing people to change or risk being punished.

What Should I Do When an HRD Program Includes Controversial Material?

You must first define what you mean by controversial. Controversies can arise in many forms, and they usually reflect an ethical dilemma. Think of an issue that might arise in your company. For example, if you were employed by a chemical company that planned to do an HRD program to train workers how to efficiently dump chemical waste into a public sewer, what would you do? How would you feel about being in a sales training program to train your people how to surreptitiously damage a competitor's product during a demonstration to a potential buyer?

As a manager, you are presumed to be endorsing and applying the values of the organization. If you do not agree with them, you can always exercise your option of leaving. Of course, exercising any option means making a choice—to stay where you do not agree with the policy or to leave and accept the consequences (perhaps a lower-level job or relocation).

The same applies to your employees. The difference is that you may be the one assigning them to the problematic HRD program. You are the one who should decide whether to send your employees to participate in a controversial HRD program. You should not force them to make that decision. (Of course, they too have the right to refuse—and accept the consequences.)

Is HRD a Form of Brainwashing?

It is not brainwashing in the usual sense, but it can be seen that way. There are times when HRD cannot provide the learner with performance options but must insist on only one way to do the job. How would you feel about riding in an airplane if the pilot had not been trained (brainwashed) in specific takeoff and landing procedures but was encouraged to do whatever he or she wanted?

If we ever reach the point where HRD uses techniques that deprive an individual of the right to make choices, then it could become a very dangerous form of brainwashing. This is not as outlandish an idea as you might think, for there are those who encourage the use of drugs and other mind-controlling approaches in HRD. That could indeed be brainwashing.

Is HRD a Form of Therapy?

Absolutely not! Therapy starts with the assumption that the individual is mentally ill. When one of your employees is mentally ill, that individual should be referred to the proper mental health resource, not HRD.

Some managers try to use HRD as a form of therapy. They may send an employee to an HRD program to "straighten him (or her) out." If "straightening out" referred to changing the employee's attitude to such things as company policies or customer relations, HRD would probably be appropriate. Otherwise, not.

When an employee has personal problems, or when family pressures induce problems, HRD is absolutely inappropriate as a response.

I Have Heard That Managers Should
Consider Their Employees to Be Volunteers.
What Does That Mean?

In some countries, employees at all levels are assigned to their jobs by the government. They have few, if any, options. In the United States, you find your own job, and you can leave it anytime you wish. In essence, then, workers in the United States at all levels have essentially "volunteered" to work for a particular employer. Sometimes there is a contract of employment for a specified number of years, but that is only because the employee and the employer have freely chosen to enter into that contract.

It is important to recognize this distinction in employment practices. If you consider employees as volunteers, you will recognize their need for encouragement and reinforcement. For HRD, it suggests that employees should be involved in planning for their training, education, and development, within the framework of what you can provide. They should have some options, when possible, rather than merely being assigned to learning programs.

Is HRD Ever Used to Fight Unions?

Unfortunately, there is a history of this. In the past, it was quite common for an employer to identify a worker who was a union leader, offer him or her a supervisory education program, and thereby take the first steps toward removing that union leader from the bargaining unit. The reaction from some unions was to take a position against all HRD programs, seeing them as having the potential for destroying union leadership.

There were also cases where certain employees with anti-union sentiments were given education so they could qualify for promotions, while strong union backers were not given similar opportunities. This contributed to the anti-HRD feeling in some unions.

Fortunately, with a combination of enlightened leadership in management and the unions and a general decline in unionization among service and technical industries, this has become much less of a concern.

How Can I Work with Unions in HRD Situations?

Think positively. If you have a union, it should be seen as a partner in HRD rather than an opponent. Consider involving appropriate union leaders in planning for HRD and even in some elements of evaluation.

This may require that your organization formulate some policies about HRD and unions. If your suggestions seem unusual, you can point to various examples of company-union cooperation in HRD. For example, Chrysler and the United Auto Workers have a joint HRD project. It started out as a way to bring minority workers into Chrysler but then was extended so that the HRD project provided HRD services to the entire company.

Should HRD Help Me Relate to My Community?

Increasingly, organizations are recognizing the need to be involved in the communities where they are located. You should first determine whether your organization has a policy that encourages employees to become involved in the community either in a personal way or as representing the company.

Many organizations have realized that they are "citizens" of a community and thus that the community's problems can also be the organization's problems. It is to their mutual interest to work together to solve problems. HRD is certainly not the whole answer, but it is a part of your organization that can be a prime force in helping you relate to your community.

How Can HRD Help Me Relate to My Community?

There is hardly a community anywhere that could not benefit from organized learning programs. Many communities utilize volunteers in a variety of community-sponsored programs, and those volunteers could use training and education. The HRD expertise in particular subjects may not exist in your company, but where there is an HRD unit, someone could certainly provide some of the learning experiences required by volunteers.

If, for example, you are called upon to be the leader (president, chair) of a community group, you may want your HRD people to assist you in improving your skills for chairing meetings, involving others, and communicating. You may already have some of those skills, but they would not be used exactly the same way in a community setting as they are in the work setting. Your HRD people should be able to help you make that transition.

Can My HRD Operation
Help Our Local School System?

The response to this question is a resounding yes. This is an area in which a great deal can be done. There are many examples of companies and individuals doing great work with school systems, but still more needs to be done, and your HRD unit should be utilized.

It is possible, for example, to arrange for an exchange of personnel. That is, an HRD person could be assigned to teach in a local school, while a teacher from that school would be assigned to your HRD unit. This should be done not to recruit that teacher out of the classroom but to help the teacher understand the world of work to which graduates might be going. It may also serve to improve the instructional skills of the teacher.

There might also be some HRD equipment that is no longer needed by your organization but could still be useful in the school setting. You might also want to check some of the tax implications of this, as they can be very beneficial to your company.

How Can the Local School
System Help My HRD Operation?

Think of the local school system as a pool of talent. For example, there may be subject matter specialists in the school system who could help your HRD people design a program. Depending on how up-to-date the school system is in your community, there might even be some faculty in that school system who are proficient in specific instructional areas, such as using computers for learning.

What Is a Cooperative Program?

Cooperative programs are familiar to engineers but less known to others. This is a type of work-study program that has been in use in the engineering field since the early 1900s. It has slowly been extended to other fields but is still inadequately used, and too often it does not involve the HRD unit.

The essential idea of the program is that college students are put into an organized program involving both study and work. A typical program would be one in which the student spends one semester in school and then one semester working in a regular job that is related to what is being studied. As a manager, you may have received cooperative program students.

How Can an HRD Unit Be
Helpful to Me in Cooperative Programs?

Your HRD people can help you to link the college with your organization and your unit. The request for a cooperative program usually originates with the educational institution, and your HRD people can help in the preliminary work of exploring the options and setting up the program for you. They can also help on the administrative side, for there is always a certain amount of paper work. This is essential to clarify the objectives of all parties concerned: your organization, the educational institution, and the students. Your HRD people can also be of assistance in planning appropriate work experiences for the students. You are usually asked to evaluate the students, and HRD can also help with that.

How Will Economic Conditions
Affect HRD in My Organization?

Economic conditions are constantly changing. When conditions are good, you can expect little pressure on you to cut costs or reduce expenditures. When there is a decline in general economic conditions (a recession or depression), organizations tend to look at what can be cut. This is necessary for survival. However, it is really not true that "training should be the first thing cut." Indeed, if your organization does that, it is bringing disaster on itself.

It is obvious that at a time of economic decline the emphasis is on those activities that contribute to survival and immediate returns. During an economic decline, development is virtually eliminated since that HRD activity does not contribute to the current success of the organization. Education will usually be reduced because there will be fewer opportunities for promotion. Education might be increased if your organization decides to use that aspect of HRD to reassign people to other units and departments. If there is sufficient time, education can be very helpful in this respect.

It is almost certain that training should be increased, for it can contribute to immediate improvement in performance, higher productivity, and reduced costs. All those elements are critical during a time of economic decline. If the distinction is not made among those three types of HRD programs, you and your organization can lose the benefits of training in across-the-board cutbacks in HRD activity.

Why Should My Organization
Provide HRD for Special Populations?

Special populations is the term that has emerged for people in the work force who have unusual needs of various kinds. These groups tend to change as a result of legislation, demographic changes, and immigration. They have included physically disabled people; mentally disabled people; minorities (as defined by law) such as blacks, Hispanics, and women; immigrants, such as those who came to the United States from Southeast Asia in large numbers in the late 1980s; and older workers.

It is possible for almost all of these special populations to be gainfully employed, thereby increasing your payrolls while reducing the welfare rolls. Providing HRD targeted to those populations can also enhance the image of your organization and indicate your recognition of social responsibility. Conversely, if you are insensitive to hiring and meeting the needs of special populations, the result could be lawsuits, a negative image, and a reduced labor pool.

How Can HRD Help Me to
Provide Learning for Special Populations?

Your HRD people should know some of the challenges associated with providing learning for special populations. For example, if you are employing immigrants in your unit, those employees will probably need learning activities designed to improve their English.

Although your HRD people may not be experienced in providing learning for mentally disabled employees, they should be able to identify the external resources that can do so, and they may be able to assist you in the program.

For minorities, special programs and materials for learning programs have been around since 1964. In addition, there are programs for supervisors who are receiving minorities in their units for the first time. Your HRD people should know of those programs and materials and be able to locate what you may need in that area.

How Can HRD Relate to Changing Demographics?

The demographics of the work force — that is, how it breaks down by age and other factors — are constantly changing. The general trends are relatively easy to discover, as that information can be purchased from the Bureau of the Census. Also, articles on demographic trends appear from time to time in the HRD literature, as well as elsewhere.

What is generally missing are the specifics on the local area from which your work force is drawn. Although there is geographical mobility in our work force, your organization is more likely to draw from existing labor pools in nearby communities for the bulk of your workers. Of course, those at higher levels of the organization, or special groups such as engineers, might be recruited from a distance.

If your organization is service oriented and serves a defined local area, your marketing people probably have all the demographic information you need. You should help create the linkage between them and your HRD people so that appropriate learning experiences can be planned for both your current employees and your potential work force. Of particular interest are two age groups, the younger worker (just entering the work force) and the older worker (generally, anyone over fifty-five years of age).

How can HRD help me with younger workers? You have probably heard a great deal about how young people are graduating from our schools without the necessary skills to function in the workplace. We need not discuss whether this is true nationwide, but you do need to be concerned about the new young workers you are receiving. Do they need remedial work in communication skills or mathematics? If so, your HRD people can help you.

For many young people there is another problem, for even if they have the skills, they may know very little of the world of work. In prior generations, they saw role models in their parents (usually their fathers), who worked near the home. As distances between the work site and the home increased, young people's knowledge of the workplace became limited to what they heard their parents say about work.

The difficulty today is that work changes very rapidly, and the way people work also changes. There has been a movement from production to service, although some young people still have parents who are part of the production environment. Many young people lack role models for service work.

That great medium of communication, the television set, provides practically no information about work. Even worse, what it presents is misleading. With all due respect to that great performer Lucille Ball, no employer would have kept her on the job given her continual ludicrous performance. It made for great television, but it may have given some young people a distorted idea of what it is to work in an office or a factory.

It may be necessary for your HRD unit to provide learning experiences for new young workers on what is appropriate behavior for success in your organization.

How can HRD help me with older workers? *Older* is, of course, a relative term. It is generally used in the United States for people over fifty-five. In other places — Singapore for example — it applies to workers over forty. It is also tied in with retirement age. Although in the United States the retirement age is still generally from sixty-two to sixty-five, this fact does not adequately represent the situation. People over sixty-five may officially retire from a job they have held for many years but still remain in the work force. Indeed, some major companies have found that their retired workers make excellent part-time workers in other parts of the same organization.

There are still too many negative stereotypes about older workers. You have undoubtedly heard the usual one about how you can't teach an old dog new tricks. That may be true for dogs, but there is absolutely no evidence that it is true for people. Your older employees can learn, but they may learn differently from younger employees. Your HRD staff can help to provide the appropriate learning experiences for your older employees.

Organizations are increasingly discovering the value of older people as employees at all levels of the organization. Research shows that their attendance tends to be better than that of younger workers, despite rumors to the contrary. They have tremendous potential, and using HRD is one way of uncovering and utilizing that potential.

Does HRD Have a Place in Stockholder Relations?

You may not be directly involved in stockholder meetings and relations, but your organization may have other mechanisms for involving investors or the community. These usually involve meetings, and HRD people can help you in planning and implementing the most effective meetings. They can also help to prepare managers in your company to serve as the chair or as a resource for those meetings.

There has been a movement for stockholders to become more active in those organizations where they hold stock. In such situations, the HRD unit could be utilized to plan training activities for stockholders to learn about their rights, their relationship to the company, and the appropriate conduct at meetings.

Should Our Organization Be Concerned About Legislation That Affects HRD?

Both Congress and legislatures at the state and local levels have increasingly been making laws that have all kinds of HRD implications. Two influential early pieces of legislation were the Economic Opportunity Act and the Equal Employment Opportunity Act, both passed in 1964.

Some organizations want to stay as far away from the federal government as possible, so there may be either a policy or practice in your organization to avoid activities that involve the government in some way. It is impossible, however, to avoid them all, for there are laws concerning employment as well as HRD. Some of the laws encourage some kinds of HRD, while other laws make some kinds of HRD more taxable than others. You will find that there are many opportunities to use the laws positively in relation to your HRD activities.

What Are Some Examples of Laws Directly Related to HRD?

This is difficult to answer, as laws are constantly changing. The examples below apply as of 1990, but you should recognize that changes are inevitable. Your HRD people should be able to keep you up-to-date on the latest legislative actions concerning HRD.

There are laws that provide special tax credits if your organization employs designated groups, provides HRD for them, and keeps them on the payroll for a stipulated period of time. Given the increased pressures from international competition, Congress has been encouraging companies that do international business to provide more HRD as a way of improving the competitive position of the U.S. work force. The possibilities include such items as special funding to U.S. universities to conduct courses for those in the international field and special tax breaks for employees who have been displaced by overseas competition.

I Have Heard Something About Tuition Reimbursement and Taxes. What Is That All About?

Tuition reimbursement means that your organization reimburses an employee for learning conducted outside your organization, usually at an institution of higher education (junior or community college, four-year college, or university). There is a special provision for tuition reimbursement in Section 127 of the Internal Revenue Code, and this provision has been a problem since 1978. Every two years since 1978 Congress has passed temporary legislation concerning tuition reimbursement, and perhaps by the time you read this the issue will be resolved. It is important to know about it, however, for it can arise again in another form or in another piece of legislation.

The law, generally, has said that if the purpose is training (as defined in this book, and similarly by the Internal Revenue Service), the reimbursement can be considered an ordinary and necessary business expense. If it is education or development, it must be considered as a fringe benefit, taxable to the employee as additional income. The major problem is that this would require your organization to deduct withholding tax on the amount reimbursed. If that is not done, your organization could be held liable for interest and penalties, which could add up to significant amounts.

In each two-year renewal, Congress has made some changes. For example, sometimes it has generally waived the reason for the learning and just said that all the HRD activities funded by tuition reimbursement are deductible by the employer. At other times it has inserted such restrictions as a limit on the amount that can be deducted or an exclusion on graduate study. This inconsistency has caused great concern and inhibited an organization's tendency to use tuition reimbursement as a way of keeping the work force technologically up-to-date. There is also concern that the current laws on tuition reimbursement could point the way to legislation more directly damaging to HRD. It is possible for the tax laws to be set up so that they promote the HRD efforts of U.S. organizations, but that will not happen without the strong support of U.S. managers.

What Are Some of the Other Issues
I Should Be Concerned About?

The issues keep changing constantly. For example, if war broke out in a foreign country, it might have an impact on work in the United States. If your organization suddenly got a contract for a military item, you might have to rapidly increase your work force, and HRD would be an essential part of that effort.

Speaking more generally, it is clear that as international competitiveness increases, there will be even more pressure on the U.S. work force. Increasing the competency of your work force is crucial, and HRD can help with that.

There are many more issues, and new ones will constantly arise. As they do, you should remember that HRD can help you meet those challenges.

The Role of HRD in a Global Work Force

What Is Meant by Global HRD?

At one time, global HRD could be equated with what was going on in other countries. That is no longer possible. Global HRD has many meanings, and some of those can be found in your own organization. "Global" does not always mean something distant from your organization. There are three different dimensions of global HRD: sending employees to other countries, selling to other countries, and having managers from another country.

How Is HRD Involved in
Sending Employees to Other Countries?

This is the most common use of HRD, and it was prevalent from just after World War II to about the early 1970s. Utilizing good HRD programs, organizations could prepare their U.S. employees to work abroad. The pace of this activity has slowed considerably, but it is still a factor. Despite all the studies and experiences, it has been found that there are still too few organizations that actually use HRD programs to prepare their employees to work in a different country and culture.

Well-organized HRD programs should include education in the culture of the host country, some basic language (needed phrases), and information on the history, political structure, customs, and expectations of the host country. One objective is, of course, to make the employee useful in the new country as soon as possible. The more effectively this is done, the less

131

possibility there is that the employee will have to return to the United States before the completion of the assignment, at an additional cost that was probably not in the budget.

Should the Families of Employees Be Included in the HRD Program?

The obvious answer is yes, but in actuality it may not always be possible, for reasons of budget, availability, and so on. Yes, it will cost more than providing HRD for just the employee, but in most foreign countries the whole family is really working. This is most true for the spouse, but frequently is also the case with the children. The whole family represents your company in the foreign land. The more the whole family knows, through a good HRD program, the sooner the employee will be working at a satisfactory level without having to be concerned with the adjustment of the rest of the family.

What, If Anything, Should We Be Doing in the Way of HRD for Employees Who Are Overseas?

That depends, in part, on the kind of support that already exists in the foreign country. If your company has a substantial group there, including local employees, some kinds of HRD programs are probably already established there. The employee from the United States should be included, as needed.

One of the difficulties often faced by employees working overseas is that they are out of touch with developments back home. You should work with your HRD people to examine the HRD programs being offered by your organization in the United States. Would any of those programs be helpful to employees overseas? After all, in most cases it is expected that those employees will return to the United States. Overseas employees may benefit from programs in such areas as supervision, management, ethics, and communications. Although some of these are traditional programs, many are constantly being redesigned to reflect changes in company policy and strategic thinking.

Given recent advances in technology, it should not be too difficult to make these programs available to overseas employees.

Some redesign may be needed if the program is geared toward a professional presenter and group work. It is not difficult to redesign most programs so that they can be self-directed and individually learned.

Does Any HRD Have to Be Provided for Returning Employees?

This is one of those areas that tends to be ignored. Many companies recognize the need for HRD programs to prepare employees to work and live in another country. Not enough recognition is given to the needs of returning employees.

A good deal of what the employee will need is just pure information and might be provided by units in your organization other than HRD. Here is a situation where it is important to do some needs analysis. You should discover what it is the returning employee *needs* to learn in order to be effective in the organization at home and what it is he or she *wants* to know in order to feel part of the organization again. Those needs and wants will vary greatly depending on (among other things) the employee's level in the organization, the length of time out of the country, the HRD programs taken while out of the country, and the position the employee will be filling upon return.

Our Company Has Operations in Other Countries. What Do Other Countries Expect of Us in the Way of HRD?

This depends on the part of the world and the specific country. If your organization has facilities in Europe, it will generally be expected that you offer HRD programs similar to those offered by comparable companies in the host country.

In less-developed countries and newly developed countries, the situation is different. (Note the word *newly*. It has become more common to refer to *un*developed countries as newly developed countries.) The expectations will vary from country to country depending on the state of economic development. They will also vary depending upon your company. Generally, high-tech companies are expected to share some of their expertise with the host country, or at least with selected organizations in that country.

Are We Expected to Provide
Training, Education, and Development?

Once again, this must be answered in terms of a given organization and a specific country, but it is possible to make some generalizations at this point. Before doing so, however, we would like to remind you of the distinction between these three kinds of HRD programs. If you do not make that distinction, you can still have large overseas HRD programs — but for the wrong reasons. This happens all too often and leads to unnecessary problems. As you will recall, training is for the *present* job, education is for a *future* job, and development is *not* specifically job related.

When is training most appropriate? The general response is that training should be provided whenever there is a need or an opportunity. However, since your organization is functioning in another country, there are other factors to be considered as well.

Your company may have set up, or be preparing to set up, operations in the host country in order to use the local work force. In many of the newly developed countries you can expect to find a work force that lacks the skills you need. If you need to get into operation fast, you should hire first and then provide training after you have your work force. Some companies have tried to meet the need for such a work force by hiring people away from other companies already there. This produces the natural result of forcing wages up.

What if my company already functions in another country. Is training still necessary? The answer here is much like the one given in earlier chapters — there is *always* a need for some kind of training. The important point is to be sure that it is relevant and useful.

We have an HRD unit in this country. Can we just ship the materials out to the other country? One of the biggest mistakes that many organizations make is to export their HRD programs. Almost any HRD program will have to be modified for use in another country. The most obvious need will be for translation whenever the learners in that other country are not fluent in English. However, just translating the materials may not be as simple as it sounds. Any language contains many idioms, and a good translation is more than just finding the right words in the bilingual dictionary.

It is also probable that some of the instructional strategies will have to be modified. The learners in the host country may have learned through the rote method, through lectures, or through other less interactive learning strategies than we use in the United States. If the HRD materials include interactive strategies, it will be necessary either to modify them or to create situations where the learners can learn how to learn in a different mode.

When is education most appropriate? As with training, it is most appropriate when there is a need. If you are a rapidly growing company in the host country, you may find that a good deal of education is needed because the pool of qualified people is not sufficient.

With education you always run the risk of losing the people after you have educated them. When organizing an HRD education program, you must be very careful to specify the job the individual will be going to. The time lag between the education and the new job should be quite short. If the learner cannot set his or her sights on a new job, then that learner might just take the newly acquired skills and knowledge to another organization in the host country.

When is development most appropriate? Development in countries outside the United States has many more implications than it has in the United States. Both in Japan (a highly developed country) and in some newly developed African countries it is expected that the employer will provide some kinds of learning just for general growth. If your organization does not provide those HRD development experiences, you could be considered uncooperative and reinforce your position as an outsider.

The kinds of development experiences provided are usually related to an employee's status in the organization, as well as to what is appropriate in that country. We recall what happened when one of us started to learn how to play the violin at the age of forty in Japan. In the United States that might produce sneers and jokes. In Japan, it evoked a very favorable response, for that kind of learning is considered appropriate development for a mature person.

If My Organization Provides
Scholarships, How Does That Fit into HRD?

As with any aspect of an HRD delivery system, the question must be related to corporate objectives. The word *scholarship* is widely used outside the United States to mean something akin to *tuition reimbursement*. Generally, it is expected that the recipient will be attending a university and will be receiving a degree. Usually, the scholarships are for study outside the host country, although not necessarily in the United States.

There are good reasons for offering scholarships. The type of learning needed may not be available in the host country, for example. If the scholarship is to the United States, then provision should be made for the learner to spend some time at the home site of your organization as part of the scholarship.

In some countries, having a degree is an essential part of being a manager or a specialist such as an engineer. You can see this in the name cards used by people in those countries, where the academic degrees earned are printed on the card.

There are times, however, when scholarships are offered for other reasons and therefore might not fit into the HRD program.

What Are Some Other Reasons Why
My Company Might Offer Scholarships?

Sometimes scholarships are offered for political reasons. That is, there is an expectation that foreign companies will offer scholarships to host country personnel as a sign of friendship. It is expected that the recipients will *not* be employees, though they could be from the families of employees. In such a situation, the scholarship program should not be considered as part of your HRD program, though your HRD people might still be helpful in running it.

In Other Countries, Do HRD Programs Have Other Implications?

In the United States, HRD is generally made available to all employees who need it. In some countries that is not the case. Even if there is a need, there may be laws and customs that prevent your organization from providing learning to certain groups designated by the host government — castes, religions, ethnic minorities, and so on.

As is to be expected, those of us from the United States have difficulty in dealing with that. If your company wants to operate in a foreign country, however, you must be willing to accept the laws and customs of that country. Because providing HRD can be the first step that will help a person move into a different category, it should not be attempted without government approval if doing so could pose a problem.

Can My Company Be Expected to Provide HRD for Nonemployees?

Some countries have recognized the power that lies behind well-formulated HRD programs. As they may lack the resources, they may expect your company to provide education (not training) for others in the work force, who might then go to work for another company. Frequently, agreements negotiated when your company starts working in a host country end up *requiring* this once the host country negotiators recognize that this is a powerful way for them to upgrade their unemployed work force.

What Is the HRD Responsibility of a Multinational Company?

In the United States, the essential HRD responsibility is to the company and its employees. When a company is located in another country, there are additional elements to be considered.

For example, it is important to respect local customs. This can range from the obvious (do not mix the sexes) to the more subtle (time and location of HRD activities). Anything that upsets the equilibrium can be viewed as suspicious by a host government. HRD ranks high in this area, as it can give people new skills and raise their expectations. It may be as basic a skill as literacy, but where a government cannot control what people read, increased literacy can pose a potential threat.

Above all, an HRD program should avoid any criticism of the local school system, whether implied or explicit. In the United States, it is common for people to criticize the school system. Such criticism has been a mainstay of public life for a century or more — at least since school opportunities were developed for all U.S. citizens. In some countries, however, access to schools may not be open to all people. Moreover, those who attend may not accept any responsibility for learning if they are assured of an income at a certain age, regardless of the level of schooling actually achieved.

What Is the Levy System?

The levy system is a method of funding HRD that may seem strange to you and your company. Although it is not found in the United States, it is common elsewhere. Its existence in a given country is related not to the level of economic development but to the political system.

Levy systems take many forms, but generally the government levies a tax on the payroll of companies employing more than a stated number of employees (usually five). Following that, there are a variety of possibilities. In some countries, your company can get some or all of its tax money back if it provides HRD programs that are approved by the government. In others, the money goes to boards or committees (some of which are industry based) that then allocate the collected funds.

Whatever the system, you and your HRD people must be aware of the tax and recovery possibilities. If your operation in the host country is large enough, the sum involved could be considerable.

How Can HRD Help a Foreign Manager
Assigned to the United States?

This is a new problem in U.S. companies. Although it began to be an issue in the early 1980s, it was not until the 1990s that it became more prominent. The change was due to more foreign companies buying into U.S. companies, as well as to foreign companies setting up in the United States.

When managers are sent from the home offices in other countries to the United States, the local HRD unit can be helpful. It can provide specific job orientation for those managers, as well as orientation to U.S. customs and traditions, as needed. Too often, those managers are sent here with little more than what they learned about the United States when they were children in school. Even if it was relevant then, many years ago, it would still need to be updated for the United States today—and HRD can help do that.

HRD in the Future:
Challenges and Changes

How Has HRD Helped in the Past?

Here we will answer this question quite generally; obviously, the experiences of your particular organization may differ. Over a century ago, with the growth of organizations and industry, HRD began to become a force in corporate life. This pattern is being repeated in many newly developed countries today. Throughout the world, the use of HRD has moved work forces from agriculture and cottage industries into factories and offices. More recently, HRD has been a significant factor in moving people into positions where they are able to use the technology that is continually exploding all around us. In times of crisis, such as a war, the efficacy of HRD becomes obvious for both the uniformed and the civilian work force.

What Can I Expect of HRD in the Future?

That depends on what you expect the future to be and how you are planning to prepare for it. If your organization does little to plan for the future, then HRD must continue to be reactive, trying to solve performance problems after they have occurred. If your organization plans for the future, then identification of future-oriented HRD activities should be part of that planning. Almost any change in an organization requires new kinds of behavior and performance, and some of these can be effectively achieved by using HRD *before* the changes take place.

Will Organizations in the Future Be Very Different?

There is already an apparent trend toward a different kind of organization, but it is not possible to say for sure that it will continue. One of the more dramatic changes is the growth of so-called flat organizations. Indeed, your organization may already have moved in that direction. The trend toward fewer hierarchical levels means fewer opportunities for promotion. Organizations are dealing with this in different ways, but generally, it means that lateral movement becomes more common than promotion. Most internal mobility of this kind can benefit from well-planned HRD programs delivered at the right time.

If your organization is considering some other configuration — and there are certainly other possibilities (task forces, project groups, intrapreneurial units) — HRD can also help your work force to move positively in those directions.

What Are Some of the Issues for the Future with Which HRD Might Be Concerned?

It is always difficult to discuss the future — it keeps changing. Therefore, this response must be limited to some of the thinking about the future at the time this book was being written. Some of the more important issues that can be identified include illiteracy in the work force, the information explosion, continued technological growth, and the one-world idea.

Illiteracy in the Work Force Has Been with Us for a While — How Might It Be Different in the Future?

It will be different mainly in that literacy campaigns will focus ever more strongly on recent immigrants and their children. In addition, you should be aware that the lack of adequate literacy among employees has become an increasingly serious problem. More and more jobs require literacy and basic work skills than ever before.

What is the relationship between immigration and literacy? The United States currently has the largest immigrant population in many decades. Many of the immigrants have difficulty with English or completely lack that competency. For the next few years, it can be expected that there will be many HRD programs in English and basic work skills as efforts are made to make those recent immigrants more employable.

It is still too early to tell about their children, some of whom are beginning to enter the work force, but they can be expected to be a greater factor in the early years of the next century. At that time, they will make up a significant proportion of the work force.

If history repeats itself, the first generation of immigrant children born in the United States will be competent in English and able to integrate into the work force with few problems in the literacy area. The difficult times will be the 1990s and the first decade of the next century, as there will still be many in the work force who are immigrants or who came here as young adults lacking the necessary language skills. In addition to the literacy problem, cultural diversity raises problems that will have to be explored, but literacy may well be the key to solving most of these problems.

What happens once immigration stops? That depends on the laws that are in effect at the time. Legislation concerning immigration (legal and illegal) is constantly changing. Each change presents the possibility of a different work force and different challenges and opportunities for managers.

Do not expect your HRD manager to be conversant with the latest changes in immigration laws. Rather, all managers should at least be generally aware of those changes and what effect they might have on the makeup of the work force.

Are all the dropouts the children of immigrants? No. A significant number of dropouts are the children of parents born in the United States. Because they do not even finish high school, they will probably lack many of the basic skills you require of your beginning employees. Therefore, unless conditions change drastically, you can expect to have this problem for years to come. It is regrettable that too many people see this as a problem that can be solved in a short time. Even if a solution to the problem is identified, it will take several years for it to have any significant effect on the dropout population.

What Is the Information Explosion?

The term *information explosion* refers to the fact that we have vastly increased our ability to provide information. It probably even exceeds our need for that much information, and consequently some prefer the term *information pollution.*

In the future, information will come from many sources, and there will be increasing pressure on managers to process that information as quickly and effectively as possible. Some of your current skills in reading and thinking may have to be reevaluated, given the pressure of the information explosion.

We Have Had a Great Deal of Technological Growth — Will It Slow Down?

There is no indication of any slowdown in technological growth or in the changes it requires. It almost seems, rather, that the pace has increased! More and more of the changes in technology are affecting relationships among people, the way work is done, the elimination and emergence of jobs, and the nature of products and services.

Once you accept the fact that changes will continue to occur, you have to explore the ways in which you need to keep current. Obviously, the learning available through HRD can be a major factor in your efforts. Even *how* that learning can be made available to you will be influenced by technological changes.

What Will Happen to the "One-World" Concept?

For many years, there was a positive reaction to the idea that we all live in one world. The space program, at one point, seemed to reinforce that idea as astronauts became the first people to see our planet whole. Then a change took place. The concept of the European Economic Community was proposed, and many European nations joined it. Other parts of the world appeared to be following a similar pattern in encouraging regional economic communities.

Slowly, however, many people are recognizing that we are indeed one world, even though we may create artificial groupings, and that whatever happens in any part of the world will have its effect on us. One example is the scheduled return of Hong Kong to China in 1997. Obviously, that political change (if it actually takes place) can be expected to bring about many economic and demographic changes in countries that do not even border China. For example, some British companies have moved their headquarters to other places, such as the Bahamas, in anticipation of 1997. They still maintain operations in Hong Kong and try to keep their movement of corporate headquarters as quiet as possible.

The exodus from Hong Kong can also be felt in Canada, which has seen a very rapid growth in the population of Vancouver, mainly from Hong Kong emigrants. Other countries feeling some of that impact include Australia and, to a much lesser extent, the United States.

If you examine almost every political change in the world, you will discover some implications for managers in the United States. This suggests that it is a responsibility of almost all managers to keep up with changes throughout the world. Generally, this has not been seen as an HRD function in an organization, but it may well be one that is about to emerge.

References

Belcher, J. G., Jr. *Productivity Plus: How Today's Best-Run Companies Are Gaining the Competitive Edge.* Houston, Texas: Gulf Publishing, 1987.

Gutteridge, T. G., and Hutcheson, P. G. "Career Development." In L. Nadler and Z. Nadler (eds.), *The Handbook of Human Resource Development.* (2nd ed.) New York: Wiley, 1990.

Knowles, M. *The Adult Learner: A Neglected Species.* (3rd ed.) Houston, Texas: Gulf Publishing, 1984.

Leibowitz, Z. B., Farren, C., and Kaye, B. L. *Designing Career Development Systems.* San Francisco: Jossey-Bass, 1986.

Nadler, D. *Feedback and Organization Development: Using Data-Based Methods.* Reading, Mass.: Addison-Wesley, 1977.

Nadler, L. *Designing Training Programs.* Reading, Mass.: Addison-Wesley, 1982.

Nadler, L., and Nadler, Z. *Corporate Human Resource Development.* New York: Van Nostrand Reinhold, 1980.

Nadler, L., and Nadler, Z. *Developing Human Resources.* (3rd ed.) San Francisco: Jossey-Bass, 1989.

Reynolds, A. "Computers and HRD." In L. Nadler and Z. Nadler (eds.), *The Handbook of Human Resource Development.* (2nd ed.) New York: Wiley, 1990.